# iPhone 15 Pro Max User Guide

The Most Complete User Manual with Tips & Tricks for Beginners
and Seniors to Master the New Apple iPhone 15 Pro Max and Latest
Hidden Features in iOS 17

## Curtis

# Campbell

**Disclaimer**

The information in this book is based on personal experience and anecdotal evidence. Although the author has made every attempt to achieve an accuracy of the information gathered in this book, they make no representation or warranties concerning the accuracy or completeness of the contents of this book. Your circumstances may not be suited to some illustrations in this book.

The author disclaims any liability arising directly or indirectly from the use of this book. Readers are encouraged to seek Medical. Accounting, legal, or professional help when required. This guide is for informational purposes only, and the author does not accept any responsibilities for any liabilities resulting from the use of this information. While every attempt has been made to verify the information provided here, the author cannot assume any responsibility for errors, inaccuracies or omission.

**Printed in the United States of America**

# Table of Contents

# INTRODUCTION

This guidebook is your all-inclusive guide to the iPhone 15 Pro Max, Apple's best smartphone that takes the iPhone experience to new heights. The book covers all the requisite features and functions of this impressive device so you can utilize your iPhone 15 Pro Max to its bursting capacity.

With the powerful A17 Pro Bionic chip, refined Super Retina XDR display, and pro-level camera system, the iPhone 15 Pro Max delivers exceptional performance for work, play, and creativity; this guide aims to help you master core phone functions like settings, apps, camera controls, and more.

We will also provide tips to care for your iPhone, troubleshoot issues, and connect with other Apple devices for a complete experience.

Whether you are new to the iPhone or upgrading from an older model, this thorough guide will allow you to appreciate all the remarkable upgrades the iPhone 15 Pro Max offers.

Let's get started with the possibilities of Apple's definitive pro phone!

# CHAPTER ONE

# Thorough Review of the iPhone 15 Pro Max

The iPhone 15 Pro Max introduces a revolutionary titanium design that combines durability and lightweight properties. This innovative design features titanium bands that envelop a substructure crafted entirely from recycled aluminum, creating a bond of exceptional strength. The aluminum framework serves a dual purpose by aiding thermal dissipation and facilitating the easy replacement of the rear glass. This refined design also showcases the Super Retina XDR display, enhanced with Always-On and ProMotion technologies for an elevated user experience.

Innovatively replacing the traditional single-function switch, the iPhone 15 Pro Max introduces the versatile Action button. This multifunctional button allows swift access to numerous features, including the camera, flashlight, Voice Memos, Focus modes, Translate, and accessibility options. You can customize this button to initiate various shortcuts, offering personalized convenience.

Powering the iPhone 15 Pro Max is the groundbreaking A17 Pro chip, a pioneer in 3-

nanometer technology. This chip delivers substantial performance enhancements compared to its predecessor, the A16 Bionic. The CPU boasts a remarkable 10% increase in speed, the Neural Engine doubles its processing capabilities, and the GPU exhibits a notable 20% boost in performance.

Notably, the new GPU incorporates hardware-accelerated ray tracing, which is four times faster than its software-based counterpart. This advancement enables smoother graphics and more immersive experiences in augmented reality (AR) gaming applications.

The A17 Pro chip also features a dedicated AV1 decoder, optimizing video streaming with improved efficiency and quality. A new USB controller raises the bar, enabling USB 3 speeds on the iPhone for the first time; this facilitates higher transfer speeds and supports video output up to 4K at 60 fps HDR.

The iPhone 15 Pro Max boasts an impressive camera system with the equivalent of seven professional lenses. The 48MP Main camera introduces a 24MP super-high-resolution default mode, delivering exceptional image quality without excessive file sizes. Users can switch between three popular focal lengths and select their preferred default. This iPhone offers the most extended optical zoom, reaching 5x at 120mm.

Enhancing photography capabilities further, the iPhone 15 Pro Max introduces a next-generation portrait mode. This mode captures sharper photos with vibrant colors and excels in low-light conditions. Users no longer need to switch to Portrait mode, as the iPhone automatically captures depth information when a person, dog, or cat is detected in the frame; this allows post-photo focus adjustments.

The device includes numerous camera features, including improved Night mode for sharper details and vivid colors, Smart HDR for lifelike skin tones, enhanced low-light video and Action mode, faster transfer speeds via an optional USB 3 cable, support for 48MP ProRAW images, ProRes video recording to external storage, a Log encoding option, and compatibility with the Academy Color Encoding System (ACES). These features cater to diverse photography and videography needs, attracting creative professionals.

Soon, the iPhone 15 Pro Max will introduce spatial video recording, enabling the capture of three-dimensional videos compatible with Apple Vision Pro. Moreover, the phone will adopt the universally accepted USB-C connector for charging and data transfer, ensuring compatibility across multiple Apple devices.

The iPhone 15 Pro Max boasts an array of wireless enhancements, including a second-generation Ultra-Wideband chip for precise location tracking in 'Find My,' Wi-Fi 6E for faster wireless speeds, Thread support for future Home app integrations, lightning-fast 5G connectivity, MagSafe and future Qi2 wireless charging capabilities, improved audio quality during phone calls, and eSIM compatibility with over 295 carriers. These upgrades strengthen connectivity and user experience, especially with features like Find My and FaceTime.

Enhancing safety features, the iPhone 15 Pro Max introduces Crash Detection, automatically identifying car accidents and contacting emergency services.

Also, Emergency SOS via satellite allows users to summon help even in areas lacking cellular or Wi-Fi coverage. Furthermore, Roadside Assistance via satellite connects you to AAA for service in remote areas without network connectivity. Initially free for two years in the U.S., this feature will later be covered by AAA membership or available as a separate service.

Demonstrating a commitment to environmental sustainability, the iPhone 15 Pro Max incorporates more recycled materials, including 100% recycled aluminum for the substructure and 100% recycled cobalt in the battery.

All magnets use 100% recycled rare earth elements, and the USB-C connector contains 100% recycled gold. The device meets Apple's stringent energy efficiency standards and is free from mercury, PVC, and beryllium.

Over 99% of its packaging consists of fiber-based materials. Apple is discontinuing using leather in all its products and introducing environmentally friendly alternatives, such as the FineWoven Case and Wallet with MagSafe, which are crafted from 68% post-consumer recycled content and have significantly lower carbon emissions than leather products.

## Unboxing and Initial Inspection

Apple's commitment to elegant and sustainable packaging continues with the iPhone 15 Pro Max. The device is nestled snugly in a precisely cut cardboard tray. As you lift the top, you'll be greeted by the stunning iPhone 15 Pro Max, with its impressive display, sleek design, and an array of cameras ready to capture your moments in high definition.

✓ A USB Type-C to Type-C cable:

Apple has been on a journey towards reducing electronic waste and environmental impact. Inside the box, you'll find a USB Type-C to Type-C cable. The woven appearance of the cable adds durability and aligns with Apple's eco-friendly initiatives. This cable allows for faster charging and data transfer speeds, ensuring you can immediately make the most of your new device.

✓ Documentation and Inserts:

Beneath the iPhone, you'll discover a small compartment containing essential documentation and inserts. While Apple has been striving to minimize paper waste, you'll still find the basics: a quick start guide, warranty information, and regulatory details. These documents are concise and straightforward, designed to help you start quickly.

✓ The ever-appreciated Apple logo sticker:

For Apple enthusiasts, finding the iconic Apple logo sticker inside the box is like discovering a treasure. This small but beloved item allows you to display your allegiance to the Apple ecosystem proudly. Whether you adorn your laptop, notebook, or any other surface with it, this sticker symbolizes your connection to the Apple community.

## Switch and Set Up Your iPhone 15 Pro Max

**Step 1:** Pressing the Power Button to Turn On the Device

Locate the power button on your iPhone 15 Pro Max. It is on the right side of the device.

Press and hold the power button until the Apple logo appears on the screen; this indicates that your iPhone is turning on. Release the button when you see the logo.

**Step 2:** Selecting Your Language and Region

Once your iPhone is turned on, you will be greeted with the "Hello" screen in various languages.

Swipe up from the bottom of the screen or press the screen to activate it.

Please choose your preferred language by tapping on it.

Next, select your region or country from the list provided.

**Step 3:** Connecting to a Wi-Fi Network

It would help if you connected to a Wi-Fi network to continue setting up your iPhone.

Your phone will list available Wi-Fi networks; tap on the network you want to connect to.

If the network is password-protected, enter the Wi-Fi password when prompted.

Wait for your iPhone to connect to the Wi-Fi network. When it's connected, you'll see a checkmark next to the network name.

**Step 4:** Setting Up or Transferring Your Apple ID

If you already have an Apple ID, tap "Sign in with Your Apple ID" and enter your Apple ID email and password.

If you don't have an Apple ID, tap "Don't have an Apple ID or forgot it?" and follow the on-screen instructions to create a new Apple ID.

If you're setting up your iPhone as a new device, follow the prompts to customize your settings, such as Siri, Screen Time, and Privacy.

If you're transferring data from an old iPhone or another device, select the option to share data and follow the instructions. You may need to use iCloud or a cable to transfer data.

Once you've completed these steps, your iPhone 15 Pro Max will be set up and ready to use.

## Understanding the New Physical Buttons

## and Ports

The iPhone 15 Pro Max has the following buttons:

- ✓ Volume up/down buttons
- ✓ Action button
- ✓ Side button
- ✓ Built-in stereo speaker
- ✓ Built-in microphone
- ✓ USB-C connector

The **Action button** is a new iPhone 15 Pro Max feature that replaces the ringer. It can be customized to perform different actions, such as launching the camera, turning on the flashlight, or putting the phone into silent mode.

# Navigating the Home Screen and Control Center

**Step 1:** Understanding the Home Screen Layout

The Home Screen is the main screen you see when you unlock your iPhone.

It consists of a grid of app icons and may have multiple pages you can swipe left or right to access.

At the bottom of the screen, you'll find the Dock, which can hold your most frequently used apps.

**Step 2:** App Icons, Folders, and Widgets

App Icons: To open an app, tap its Home Screen icon.

Folders: You can organize apps into folders. To create a folder, tap and hold an app until it starts wiggling, then drag it onto another app. Give the folder a name; you can add more apps by dragging them into the folder.

Widgets: Widgets provide quick access to app information. Swipe right on the Home Screen or press and hold an app icon, then tap "Edit Home Screen" to add widgets. Tap the "+" icon at the top left to add a widget, then select the widget you want and tap "Add Widget."

**Step 3:** Accessing and Customizing the Control Center

The Control Center panel provides quick access to essential settings and functions.

To access it, swipe down from the top-right corner of the screen (on iPhone with Face ID) or swipe up from the bottom of the screen (on iPhone with a Home button).

You can customize the Control Center by going to "Settings" > "Control Center." Here, you can add or remove controls, rearrange them, and customize the toggles in the Control Center.

**Step 4:** Swiping Gestures for Navigation

Swiping down from the top-right corner will take you back to the Home Screen from any app or screen.

Swipe horizontally along the screen's bottom edge to switch between recently used apps.

Swipe down from the top-left corner to the Notification Center to view notifications.

Swipe down from the center for the Search screen.

## Syncing Data and Accounts

Access Settings: Swipe down from the top-right corner of the screen to open the Control Center. Tap the gear-shaped **"Settings"** icon.

Sign in with Apple ID: Scroll down and tap **"Sign in to your iPhone"** or **"Sign in to your device."** If you don't have an Apple ID, you can create one here.

Enter Apple ID: Enter your Apple ID and password. If you don't have one, tap **"Don't have an Apple ID or forgot it?"** to create a new one or recover your password.

iCloud Setup: Once signed in, tap your Apple ID at the top of the Settings menu. Then, tap **"iCloud."**

Select What to Sync: In the iCloud settings, you can choose what data to sync to iCloud, such as Photos, Contacts, Notes, etc. Toggle the switches to enable syncing for your desired items.

1. Syncing Contacts, Photos, and Emails:

Contacts: If you've enabled iCloud Contacts sync, your contacts will automatically sync to iCloud. To check, go to **Settings > Contacts > Accounts** and ensure iCloud is selected.

Photos: Go to **Settings > Photos > iCloud Photos** to sync photos. Turn on iCloud Photos to upload your pictures and videos to iCloud.

Emails: For email, open the **"Mail"** app. Tap **"Accounts"** and select your email account. Make sure the account is set to sync. You can adjust email sync settings in the account settings.

2. Linking Social Media Accounts (if desired):

Social Media Apps: Download and open your social media apps (e.g., Facebook, X, formerly Twitter, Instagram) from the App Store.

Login: Sign in to your social media accounts within the respective apps.

Integration: Some apps may offer integration with iOS features. For example, you can link your Facebook or X account in **Settings > Facebook/X.**

3. Managing Data Synchronization Preferences:

Data & Privacy: In **Settings,** go to **"Privacy."** Here, you can control app permissions for data access, such as location, contacts, photos, etc.

App-Specific Settings: Individual apps often have their settings for data synchronization. You can access these settings within the app. For instance, in the Facebook app, you can control what data it can access and sync.

# Setting Up Face ID

Access Settings: Swipe down from the top-right corner of the screen to open the Control Center. Tap the gear-shaped **"Settings"** icon.

Face ID & Passcode: Tap **"Face ID & Passcode."** You'll need to enter your current passcode if you have one.

Set Up Face ID: Tap **"Set Up Face ID."** Follow the on-screen instructions to position your face within the frame and move your head in a circle as prompted; this will scan your face.

Complete Setup: Once the scanning is successful, tap **"Done"** to complete the Face ID setup.

Setting Up a Passcode or PIN for Security:

1. Access Settings: If you haven't already, open the **"Settings"** app as mentioned above.
2. Face ID & Passcode: Tap **"Face ID & Passcode."**

3. Enter Passcode: If you haven't set up a passcode yet, you'll be prompted to create one. If you already have one, you'll need to enter it.

4. Set Passcode: Follow the on-screen instructions to create a passcode. You can choose between a 4-digit numeric code or a custom alphanumeric code. For added security, it's recommended to use a longer passcode.

Configuring Face ID or Passcode Preferences:

1. Face ID Settings: In the **"Face ID & Passcode"** settings, you can customize Face ID preferences. You can deactivate or activate Face ID for functions like iPhone Unlock, App Store purchases, and more.

2. Change Passcode: To change your passcode, tap **"Change Passcode"** within the **"Face ID & Passcode"** settings. You'll need to enter your current passcode first.

3. Passcode Options: If you prefer a more complex passcode, tap **"Passcode Options"** when setting or changing your passcode. You can choose a custom numeric or alphanumeric code.

Importance of Device Security:

Device security is crucial to protect your data and privacy and prevent unauthorized access to your iPhone. Here's why it's essential:

✓ Privacy Protection: Passcodes and Face ID ensure that only authorized users can access your device, keeping your personal information safe.

✓ Data Security: Your iPhone contains sensitive data like emails, photos, and financial information. A passcode or Face ID adds an extra layer of security to prevent data breaches.

✓ Lost or Stolen Device: If your device is lost or stolen, a passcode or Face ID makes it difficult for unauthorized individuals to access your information.

✓ Secure Transactions: Face ID and passcodes are used for fast payments and app purchases, preventing unauthorized transactions.

✓ Identity Theft Prevention: Strong device security helps protect you from identity theft and fraud.

## Configuring Basic Settings

Access Display & Brightness: Open the **"Settings"** app.

Display & Brightness: Tap **"Display & Brightness."**

Adjust Brightness: Drag the brightness slider left or right to decrease or increase screen brightness.

Auto-Brightness: To enable automatic brightness adjustment based on your surroundings, toggle **"Auto-Brightness."**

Text Size and Bold Text: Under "Display & Brightness," you can adjust text size and enable bold text if needed.

Configuring Sound and Vibration Settings:

Access Sound & Haptics: In the **"Settings"** app, scroll down and tap **"Sound & Haptics."**

- ✓ Volume Control: Adjust the volume slider to control the overall volume of your device.
- ✓ Vibrate on Ring/Silent: You can choose whether your iPhone vibrates in Silent or Ring mode by toggling the respective switches.
- ✓ Ringtone and Alert Tones: Customize your ringtone and alert tones by tapping **"Ringtone"** or **"Text Tone"** and selecting from the available options or purchasing new ones.

Setting Up Notifications and Alerts:

- ✓ Access Notifications: In the **"Settings"** app, scroll down and tap **"Notifications."**
- ✓ App Notifications: Choose an app from the list to customize its notification settings. You can

turn notifications on or off, set notification sounds, and choose how messages are displayed.

✓ Emergency Alerts: Under "Notifications," you can configure alerts like AMBER Alerts and Emergency Alerts.

Personalizing Your Wallpaper and Display Settings:

1. Access Wallpaper: In the **"Settings"** app, tap **"Wallpaper."**

2. Choose Wallpaper: You can choose a new wallpaper for your Lock Screen, Home Screen, or both. Select **"Choose a New Wallpaper"** to browse through options.

3. Dynamic and Stills: Pick from dynamic, stills, or your photos. Preview and select the wallpaper you prefer.

4. Set Wallpaper: After selecting a wallpaper, tap **"Set"** to choose whether it should be set for the Lock Screen, Home Screen, or both.

5. Perspective Zoom: You can turn **"Perspective Zoom"** on or off for the chosen wallpaper. It

adds a subtle parallax effect when you tilt your device.

## Backing Up Your iPhone 15 Pro Max

Access iCloud Settings: Open the **"Settings"** app on your iPhone.

Your Name: Tap **your name at the top** to access your Apple ID settings.

iCloud: Tap **"iCloud."**

iCloud Backup: Scroll down and tap **"iCloud Backup."**

Toggle On: Ensure the "iCloud Backup" toggle is switched on. Your iPhone will automatically back up when connected to Wi-Fi and plugged in, and the screen is locked.

Why Regular Backups?

Regular backups ensure that your data is safe and can be restored if your device is lost, damaged, or needs replacement. It's essential for preserving photos, messages, apps, and settings.

Manually Initiating a Backup:

While automatic backups are recommended, you can manually trigger a backup anytime:

iCloud Backup: Go to **"Settings" > "Your Name" > "iCloud" > "iCloud Backup."** Tap **"Back Up Now."** Ensure you're connected to Wi-Fi and have sufficient iCloud storage.

How to Restore from a Backup if Needed:

If you ever need to restore your iPhone from a backup, follow these steps:

1. Erase All Content and Settings: Go **to "Settings" > "General" > "Reset" > "Erase All Content and Settings;"** this will wipe your device.

2. Setup Assistant: After erasing, your iPhone will restart and show the **"Hello"** screen. Follow the on-screen instructions until you reach the **"Apps & Data"** screen.

25

3. Restore from iCloud Backup: Select **"Restore from iCloud Backup."**

4. Sign In: Enter your Apple ID and password.

Choose Backup: Select the most relevant backup from the list of available backups. Ensure it contains the data you want to restore.

Restore: The restore process will begin; this may take some time, depending on the backup size and your Wi-Fi connection.

Complete Setup: After the restore is full, follow the remaining on-screen setup instructions. Your iPhone will be restored to the state of the selected backup.

# CHAPTER TWO

# Multitasking Features of the Dynamic

# Island

"Dynamic Island," a unique, pill-shaped space housing the iPhone's front camera and various sensors. This innovative element enhances your online experience, allowing seamless app navigation without needing to close or switch between tabs.

Dynamic Island serves a multitude of purposes. Whether checking the status of your AirPods connection, muting them, or even charging, each function is distinct and easily recognizable. You can also swiftly verify your Face ID or confirm your iPhone's login status while on the move. Dynamic Island is ever-present, providing real-time access to pertinent information and imbuing a sense of vitality into your device.

But what's happening in the background? Within Dynamic Island, background activities are showcased. For instance, if music plays in the background and you swipe to return to the home screen, the music app seamlessly transforms into Dynamic Island, remaining active and visible.

Music enthusiasts will appreciate the inclusion of album art. Interactivity abounds within Dynamic Island, offering additional options through simple taps or a swift return to your app.

The convenience extends further as you can access controls from Dynamic Island without exiting your current app, even during phone calls.

The tactile and visual experience is paramount in Dynamic Island's design. Apple has ensured a fluid and cohesive interaction regardless of the app from which alerts or notifications originate. In cases of multiple background activities, Dynamic Island adapts, gracefully accommodating multiple elements when necessary.

## Using Crash Detection

Activating Crash Detection on the iPhone 15 Pro Max is prudent for your safety. As its name implies, this feature is designed to identify car accidents and promptly notify authorities, potentially being a lifesaver. This safety functionality underscores one of the distinctive advantages iPhones offer over their competitors.

While switching Crash Detection on your iPhone is crucial for your safety, there may be occasions when you wish to deactivate it.

This feature can be pretty sensitive, triggering emergency calls when someone experiences a fall during extreme sports or activities where the phone might endure jostling.

Suppose you're partaking in pursuits such as skiing, skateboarding, or even riding bumper cars. In that case, it's advisable to disable Crash Detection temporarily.

However, it's strongly recommended to re-enable it once you've completed the activity to ensure ongoing safety.

Interested in knowing how to toggle Crash Detection on or off your iPhone? Follow these straightforward steps:

1. Navigate to **Settings > Emergency SOS.**
2. Locate the option labeled **"Call After Serious Crash."**

3. Depending on your preference, activate or deactivate this feature.

4. A pop-up will show up. If you're turning it off, press **"Turn off."**

## Understanding Apple Trade-In

Apple's Trade-In program is a convenient and environmentally friendly way to upgrade to a new Apple device while getting credit for your old one. It's designed to help you offset the cost of your new purchase by trading in your existing Apple product.

1. Eligibility

The Trade-In program typically covers a wide range of Apple products, including iPhones, iPads, Macs, Apple Watches, and more. Eligibility and trade-in values may vary depending on the model, condition, and market demand.

## 2. Assessment

Visit Apple's official website or an Apple Store to begin the trade-in process. You'll be asked to provide details about your current device, including its model, specifications, and condition.

Apple will assess the information you provide to determine the trade-in value of your device. The value can vary based on the device's age, condition, and current market value.

## 3. Device Collection

If you're satisfied with the trade-in value offered, you can mail your old device to Apple or bring it to an Apple Store.

Apple provides clear instructions for packaging and shipping your device securely.

## 4. Inspection

Once Apple receives your device, they will inspect it to ensure it matches the condition and specifications you provided during the assessment.

You will receive the agreed-upon trade-in credit if the device matches the description.

5. Credit Applied

The trade-in credit is typically applied toward the purchase of your new Apple product. You can use it to reduce the cost of your new device or any other Apple accessories or services.

6. Recycling

Suppose your old device is no longer in working condition or doesn't meet the criteria for a trade-in. In that case, Apple will recycle it responsibly and environmentally.

**Tips:**

- ✓ Be accurate when describing your device's condition and specifications during the assessment to ensure you receive the expected trade-in value.
- ✓ It's a good idea to back up your data and erase your old device before trading it in.

✓ Trade-In values may vary over time, so it's a good practice to check the current value of your device before initiating the trade-in process.

# CHAPTER THREE

# Using Apple Map

Tap the **"Maps"** icon on your iPhone's home screen to open Apple Maps. It looks like a folded map.

✓ Search for a Location:

Tap the **search bar** at the top of the screen.

Type in the name of the place, address, or even a general search term like "coffee."

As you type, suggestions will appear. Tap the one that matches your search.

✓ Get Directions:

Once you've searched for a location, tap on it in the search results.

Tap the **"Directions"** button.

Choose "Drive," "Walk," "Transit," or "Ride" based on your mode of transportation.

✓ Start Navigation:

Tap the **"Start"** button, and Apple Maps will provide turn-by-turn directions.

✓ Navigate with Voice Directions:

Follow the on-screen instructions and listen to voice directions to reach your destination.

You can control the volume of voice directions by using the volume buttons on your iPhone.

✓ Zoom and Pan:

Pinch or spread two fingers on the map to zoom in or out.

Swipe with one finger to pan the map in different directions.

✓ Search Along the Route:

While navigating, you can tap the search bar to find gas stations, restaurants, or other points of interest along your route.

✓ Avoid Tolls and Highways (Optional):

Tap the **"Options"** button when setting up directions and toggle on the desired options to avoid tolls or highways during your route.

✓ End Navigation:

When you've reached your destination, tap the **"End"** button at the top left of the screen.

✓ Features:

Apple Maps offers various features like 3D views of cities, indoor maps of malls and airports, and real-time transit information (where available). Learn these features by searching for specific locations or using the **"Explore"** tab.

✓ Save Favorite Locations:

You can save frequently visited places by tapping on the location pin and then tapping **"Add to Favorites."** These will be accessible under the **"Favorites"** tab.

✓ Share Your ETA:

While navigating, you can tap the **"Share ETA"** option to send your estimated arrival time to someone via Messages.

## Get Started with the Health App

Getting started with the Health app on your iPhone 15 Pro Max is a great way to track and manage your health and fitness data.

1. Open the Health App:

Locate the **Health app** on your iPhone. It's a white app icon with a red heart inside.

2. Set Up Health Profile:

Opening the app for the first time will ask you to create a health profile. Enter your personal information, like birthdate, sex, and weight. This information is essential for accurate health tracking.

3. Health Categories:

The Health app is organized into several categories, such as "Activity," "Nutrition," "Sleep," "Vitals," and more. Each type focuses on specific health data.

4. Add Data Manually:

To start tracking your health data, tap on a category that interests you, like **"Activity."**

You can add data manually by tapping the **"+"** sign in the top right corner. For example, you can manually enter your steps, workouts, or dietary information.

5. Connect Apps and Devices:

The Health app can gather data from other health and fitness apps and compatible devices. To connect them, tap **"Browse"** in the bottom right corner.

You can browse and select apps and devices you want to integrate with the Health app. For example, if you use a fitness tracker, you can connect it here.

6. Health Records:

You can access your health records in the Health app, including medical records, lab results, and more. Tap on **"Health Records"** to set this up if available.

7. Health Categories:

Take time to understand the various health categories in the app. You can track your daily steps, monitor your heart rate, record your sleep patterns, and more.

## 8. Set Goals:

To help you stay motivated, you can set health goals within the app. For instance, you can set a daily step goal or aim to get a certain amount of exercise each week.

## 9. View Health Dashboard:

The app's main "Today" tab provides a dashboard with an overview of your daily health data. Here, you can see your progress towards your goals.

## 10. Customize Health Data:

You can customize the data on your dashboard by tapping **"Edit"** in the top right corner. Add or remove specific metrics to tailor it to your preferences.

## 11. Privacy and Data Sharing:

Apple places a strong emphasis on privacy. You have control over what data is collected and how it's shared. If you choose to sync, your health data is encrypted and stored securely on your device or in iCloud.

12. Review and Share Data:

Over time, the Health app will accumulate valuable health data. You can review this data, generate reports, and share it with healthcare providers.

## Apple Translate

The Apple Translate app on your iPhone 15 Pro Max can help you communicate in different languages.

1. Open the Translate App

Locate the **"Translate"** app on your iPhone. It's a globe-like icon with a white and blue speech bubble.

2. Choose Languages

You'll see two language boxes at the top when you open the app. Tap the language in the left box to select the language you want to translate from and tap the language in the right box to choose the language you want to translate to.

## 3. Translation Modes

The Translate app offers two modes: **"Conversation"** and **"Single."**

Conversation Mode: This mode is helpful for real-time conversations. Each person can speak, and the app will translate their words into the selected language.

Single Mode: In this mode, you can type or speak a sentence, and the app will provide the translation.

## 4. Conversation Mode

If you're using Conversation Mode, tap the microphone icon for your language. Speak your sentence, and the app will translate it into another language. Then, the other person can respond in their language, and the app will translate their response back to you.

## 5. Single Mode

In Single Mode, you can type or speak a sentence or phrase you want to translate. Tap the microphone icon and talk, or type your sentence into the text field, and the app will provide the translation.

## 6. Pronunciation

To hear the pronunciation of the translated phrase, tap the **play button** next to the translated text.

## 7. Saved Translations

The app automatically saves your recent translations, making it easy to refer back to them. You can access your translation history by tapping the **"History"** button.

## 8. Favorites

You can mark translations as favorites by tapping the **star icon;** this is useful for saving commonly used phrases.

## 9. Offline Translation

The Translate app can work offline for downloaded languages. Tap the **download button** next to the language name in the language selection screen to download a language for offline use.

## 10. Privacy

Apple emphasizes privacy in the Translate app. Your translations are processed on your device, and Apple does not store your data.

## 11. Auto-Detect Language

The app can auto-detect if you're unsure what language you're hearing or reading. Just tap the **microphone icon** without selecting a specific language.

## 12. Dark Mode

The app supports Dark Mode for nighttime or low-light use. It will automatically switch if your device is set to Dark Mode.

## Pairing AirPods

Ensure that your AirPods have some charge by placing them in the charging case for a while.

Open the AirPods Case:

1. Open the lid of the AirPods case. The AirPods should be inside.
2. Enable Bluetooth on Your iPhone:
3. On your iPhone, swipe down from the top-right corner of the screen to open the Control Center. Alternatively, go to **"Settings" > "Bluetooth"** and toggle it on.

Put AirPods in Pairing Mode:

With the AirPods case open and the AirPods inside, press and hold the button on the back until the LED indicator on the front starts flashing white; this indicates that the AirPods are in pairing mode.

Connect AirPods to iPhone:

1. On your iPhone, a pop-up window should appear with an image of your AirPods and a **"Connect"** button. Tap "Connect."

2. If the pop-up window doesn't appear, go to **"Settings" > "Bluetooth,"** and you should see your AirPods listed. Tap on them to initiate the pairing.

Complete the Pairing:

A window will appear showing the connection status of your AirPods. Once the pairing is complete, you'll see **"Connected"** on the screen.

Configure Settings:

1. After pairing, you can customize your AirPods settings. Tap "Done" on the pairing confirmation screen, or go to **"Settings" > "Bluetooth" >** tap the **"i"** icon next to your AirPods name.

2. Here, you can configure options like automatic ear detection, double-tap actions, microphone preferences, and more.

Test Your AirPods:

Put both AirPods in your ears and play music or a podcast to ensure they're working correctly.

Use Siri:

If you have the new second-generation AirPods Pro, you can use the "Hey Siri" voice command to control your AirPods hands-free. Just say, "Hey Siri," followed by your command.

## Pairing Apple Watch

Make sure your iPhone and Apple Watch are close to each other.

✓ Turn on Your Apple Watch:

Press and hold the side button (located below the Digital Crown) on your Apple Watch until the Apple logo appears.

✓ Choose Language and Region:

On your Apple Watch, you'll see a screen prompting you to select your language and region. Swipe up or down to make your choices.

✓ Open the Watch App on iPhone:

On your iPhone, open the **"Watch"** app. If you can't find it, use the Search feature to locate it.

Tap "Start Pairing":

In the Watch app on your iPhone, tap **"Start Pairing."**

✓ Scan the Animation on Your Watch:

Your iPhone will display an animation with a pattern of blue particles. Hold your Apple Watch over this animation so your watch's camera can scan it.

✓ Pairing Process:

When the scanning is successful, you'll see a message on your iPhone saying, **"Your Apple Watch is Paired."** Tap **"Continue."**

✓ Set Up Your Apple Watch:

Follow the on-screen instructions on your iPhone to set up your Apple Watch; this includes choosing whether you want to restore from a backup or set up as a new watch, signing in with your Apple ID, and accepting terms and conditions.

✓ Create a Passcode:

You can set up a passcode on your Apple Watch for added security. This passcode can be different from your iPhone's passcode.

✓ Choose Settings and Apps:

Follow the prompts to customize settings such as wrist preference, app installation preferences, and whether you want to share app analytics with Apple.

✓ Set Up Activity:

You'll have the option to set up Activity on your Apple Watch, including setting daily movement goals.

✓ Install Apps:

If you've chosen to install apps, your Apple Watch will begin downloading and installing compatible apps from your iPhone.

Syncing Process:

The syncing process may take a few minutes. Once it's complete, your Apple Watch will be ready to use.

✓ Navigate Your Apple Watch:

Put your Apple Watch on your wrist and go through its features. Swipe, tap, and use the Digital Crown to navigate.

✓ Additional Apps:

If needed, you can install additional apps directly from the App Store on your Apple Watch.

# CarPlay Integration

Using Apple CarPlay with your iPhone 15 Pro Max is a convenient way to integrate your iPhone's features and apps with your car's infotainment system.

✓ Ensure CarPlay Compatibility:

First, check if your car's infotainment system supports Apple CarPlay. Many newer vehicles offer CarPlay compatibility, but not all do.

✓ Connect Your iPhone:

Connect your iPhone to your car's infotainment system using your USB cable. Ensure the cable is compatible and in good condition.

✓ Unlock Your iPhone:

Unlock your iPhone using Face ID or your passcode.

✓ Enable CarPlay on Your Car's Display:

Your car's infotainment system should detect the connected iPhone and prompt you to enable

CarPlay. Follow the on-screen instructions on your car's display.

✓ Access CarPlay Features:

Once CarPlay is enabled, your car's screen will display the CarPlay interface, which resembles the familiar iPhone home screen.

✓ Navigate CarPlay Interface:

You can navigate the CarPlay interface using touchscreen controls, physical knobs, or buttons on your car's infotainment system—familiar iPhone gestures like swiping, tapping, and pinching work here.

✓ Use CarPlay Apps:

CarPlay supports a variety of apps, including Maps, Phone, Messages, Music, Podcasts, and third-party apps like Spotify, Apple/Google Maps, and WhatsApp (if installed on your iPhone). Tap the app icons to access and use them.

✓ Use Siri Hands-Free:

CarPlay allows you to use Siri hands-free by pressing and holding the voice control button on your steering wheel or using the "Hey Siri" voice command. You can ask Siri for directions, send messages, make calls, and control music.

✓ Get Directions with Apple Maps:

Use Apple Maps for turn-by-turn navigation. Enter your destination by tapping on Maps or using Siri voice commands.

✓ Make Calls and Send Messages:

You can make calls and send messages through CarPlay. Use Siri to make calls or dictate messages to keep your hands on the wheel.

✓ Control Music and Audio:

Access your music library, playlists, and streaming apps like Apple Music or Spotify through CarPlay—control playback using the touchscreen or voice commands.

✓ Customize CarPlay:

To customize CarPlay, open the Settings app on your iPhone and scroll down to **"CarPlay."** Here, you can arrange the app icons, turn apps on or off, and customize settings for your CarPlay experience.

✓ Exit CarPlay:

To exit CarPlay and return to your car's native infotainment system, unplug your iPhone or use the exit button on your car's display.

## Connecting Apple TV

✓ Ensure Wi-Fi and Bluetooth are Enabled:

On your iPhone 15 Pro Max, ensure that Wi-Fi and Bluetooth are turned on.

✓ Connect to the Same Wi-Fi Network:

In communicating, your iPhone and Apple TV must be connected to the same Wi-Fi network. Please make sure they are on the same network.

✓ Wake Up Apple TV:

Ensure that your Apple TV is awake and on the home screen. If it's asleep, press any button on the Apple TV remote to wake it up.

✓ Use AirPlay (Screen Mirroring or Content Sharing):

Screen Mirroring: If you want to mirror your iPhone screen on the Apple TV, swipe down from the upper-right corner of your iPhone to open the Control Center. Tap **"Screen Mirroring"** and select your Apple TV from the list. You may need to enter a code on your TV screen to confirm.

Content Sharing: To share specific content (e.g., photos, videos, music) from your iPhone to the Apple TV, open the app containing the content (e.g., Photos or Videos). Look for the AirPlay icon (a rectangle with an upward-facing arrow) within the app. Tap it, and select your Apple TV from the list of available devices.

✓ Control Apple TV with Your iPhone (Apple TV Remote):

Download the **"Apple TV Remote"** app from the App Store if you haven't already.

Ensure your iPhone is on the same Wi-Fi network as your Apple TV.

Open the **"Apple TV Remote"** app and tap **"Add Apple TV."** Select your Apple TV from the list.

Follow the on-screen instructions to pair your iPhone with the Apple TV. You may need to enter a code on your TV screen to complete the setup.

Once paired, you can use your iPhone as a remote control for the Apple TV, including navigating menus, entering text, and using Siri voice commands.

✓ Control Apple TV with Control Center:

You can also use the Control Center on your iPhone to control playback and navigate within apps like Apple Music or YouTube on the Apple TV. Swipe down from the upper-right corner of your iPhone's screen to access Control Center, and tap the Apple TV icon to access playback controls.

## Setting Up the Podcast App

On your iPhone, look for the **"Podcasts"** app icon. It's a purple icon with a microphone.

✓ Open the Podcasts App:

Tap the "Podcasts" icon to open the app.

✓ Study the Welcome Screen:

You'll see a welcome screen if you're opening the Podcasts app for the first time. You can browse featured podcasts and get recommendations. You can also tap **"Continue"** to proceed to the main interface.

✓ Search for Podcasts:

To find specific podcasts or browse different categories, tap the **"Search"** tab at the bottom right (it looks like a magnifying glass).

Use the search bar at the top to enter keywords or the name of a podcast you want to find.

Browse categories by tapping "Browse" at the bottom of the screen to discover podcasts by genre.

✓ Subscribe to Podcasts:

When you find a podcast you like, tap on it to view its details.

Tap the **"Subscribe"** button to subscribe to the podcast. Subscribing means new episodes will be automatically downloaded or added to your library when released.

✓ Listen to Podcasts:

After subscribing to a podcast, go to the **"Library"** tab at the bottom of the screen to access your podcast subscriptions.

Tap on a podcast to see its episodes. Tap an episode to start listening.

✓ Download Episodes:

Tap the cloud icon next to the episode if you prefer to download episodes for offline listening; this will download it to your device.

✓ Manage Your Library:

You can organize your library by creating playlists, marking episodes as played, or removing episodes you've finished.

✓ Customize Settings:

Go to the **"Settings"** tab at the bottom right to access app settings. Here, you can adjust playback speed, choose whether to download episodes on Wi-Fi only, and more.

✓ Subscribe and Listen:

Repeat the process to find, subscribe to, and listen to more podcasts. The app will keep track of your subscriptions and play history.

✓ Additional Features:

The Podcasts app offers features like personalized recommendations, the ability to create playlists, and the option to share episodes with friends.

# CHAPTER FOUR

# Using FaceTime and Animoji

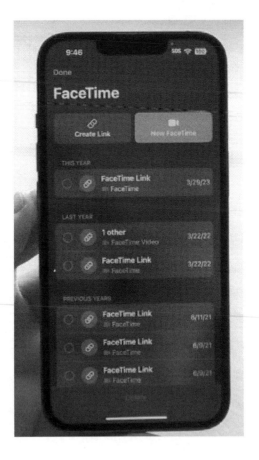

Open FaceTime: Locate the **FaceTime app** on your iPhone 15 Pro Max (it has a green icon with a white camera). Tap to open it.

Choose Recipient: To make a call, tap the **"+"** button in the top-right corner and enter the contact's name, phone number, or email address. Alternatively, tap an existing contact from your list.

Select Video or Audio Call: Click the respective icon to choose between a video or audio call. For video calls, your front or rear camera will activate.

Place the Call: Tap the green call button to initiate the call. Wait for the recipient to answer.

✓ Setting Up and Managing FaceTime Preferences:

Open Settings: Go to your iPhone's **"Settings."**

Scroll Down: Scroll down and tap **"FaceTime."**

Configure Preferences: Here, you can turn FaceTime on or off, set your caller ID, and choose whether you want FaceTime to use cellular data (if Wi-Fi is unavailable).

✓ Using Animoji and Memoji During Calls:

Open FaceTime: Start a FaceTime call, as previously mentioned.

Access Effects: While on the call, tap the star-shaped icon.

Choose Animoji or Memoji: Scroll through the available Animoji and Memoji characters and tap one to select it.

Interact with Animoji/Memoji: Your chosen character will mimic your facial expressions and speech in real-time. You can use this to add fun and personality to your calls.

✓ Group FaceTime Calls and Screen Sharing:

Group FaceTime Calls: To start a group FaceTime call, open the FaceTime app, tap the **"+"** button, and add multiple contacts. You can simultaneously have video or audio group calls with up to 32 people.

Screen Sharing: Tap the screen to reveal call options during a FaceTime call. Tap the **"Share Play"** button, which looks like a rectangle with an arrow. You can share your screen with others during the call, making it useful for presentations or showing something on your device.

## Apple Pay and Wallet

Apple Pay and Wallet make it easy to make secure payments, manage cards, and access digital passes and tickets, simplifying your financial transactions and offering convenience for in-person and online purchases.

Open Wallet: On your iPhone 15 Pro Max, find and open the **"Wallet"** app.

Add a Card: To add a card to Apple Pay, tap the **"+"** button. You can choose to add a credit or debit card.

Follow On-screen Instructions: The app will guide you through the setup process. You can either manually enter your card details or use your iPhone's camera to scan the card.

Verify Your Card: Depending on your bank, you might need to verify your card by receiving a verification code via text, email, or a phone call.

Agree to Terms: Read and agree to the terms and conditions.

Complete Setup: Once the card is added and verified, it will be available with Apple Pay.

✓ Making Contactless Payments in Stores:

Unlock Your iPhone: Double-click the side button (on the right side of your iPhone) or use Face ID if enabled to authenticate yourself.

Hold Your iPhone Near the Contactless Reader: Close your iPhone to the contactless payment terminal. Ensure it's close enough for the NFC (Near Field Communication) to work.

Authenticate: Use Face ID or your device passcode to confirm the payment. Your iPhone will provide feedback when the payment is successful.

✓ Using Apple Pay for Online and In-App Purchases:

Online Purchases: When shopping online, choose Apple Pay as your payment method at checkout. Verify your payment using Face ID or device passcode.

In-App Purchases: For in-app purchases, select Apple Pay as the payment option within the app. Follow the on-screen instructions to complete the purchase.

✓ Managing Loyalty Cards and Passes in Wallet:

Loyalty Cards: Some stores and restaurants offer digital loyalty cards. These can be added to the Wallet app by tapping the "+" button and selecting **"Loyalty Card."** Scan the barcode or QR code on the physical card, which will be added to your Wallet.

Boarding Passes and Tickets: When you receive electronic boarding passes or event tickets via email, you can often add them to your Wallet by tapping **"Add to Apple Wallet"** in the email; this is convenient for quick access without searching through your emails.

Organizing Passes: You can organize passes in the Wallet app by tapping **"Edit Passes;"** this allows you to rearrange, delete, or manage your stored keys.

## AirDrop and Sharing

AirDrop is a convenient way to quickly share files, photos, and links between Apple devices.

Open the Content: Start by opening the file, photo, or link you want to share on your iPhone.

Access the Share Menu: Tap the **"Share"** button or icon within your app; this usually looks like a box with an upward arrow.

Select AirDrop: You'll see the AirDrop option in the Share menu. Tap it to proceed.

Choose Recipient: Your iPhone will search for nearby devices with AirDrop enabled. When you see the name or device icon of the recipient you want to share with, tap their name to select them.

Send: After selecting the recipient, tap **"Send"** or **"Share"** to initiate the transfer. The recipient will receive a notification asking if they want to accept the AirDrop.

Accept the AirDrop (Recipient): The recipient needs to accept the AirDrop by tapping **"Accept"** or **"Decline."** If they accept, the content will be transferred to their device.

✓ Configuring AirDrop Settings and Visibility:

Open Control Center: Swipe down from the upper-right corner of your iPhone screen to open Control Center.

Access AirDrop Settings: Press and hold the connectivity box (top-left corner), which shows options like Wi-Fi and Bluetooth; this will expand the menu.

Set AirDrop Visibility: Here, you can choose your AirDrop visibility:

Receiving Off: No one can see your device.

Contacts Only: Only your contacts can see your device.

Everyone: All nearby devices with AirDrop enabled can see your device.

✓ Sharing Content with Nearby Devices:

Nearby Sharing: You can use the "Nearby Share" feature. Open the content you want to share, tap the **"Share"** button, and select **"Nearby Share."** Nearby devices will appear, and you can choose the recipient.

Sharing via Messages and Other Apps:

Sharing via Messages: You can easily share content through the Messages app. Open the Messages app, start a conversation, and tap the **camera icon** to share photos or files. You can also paste links directly into the chat.

Sharing via Other Apps: Most apps allow you to share content within them. Look for the **"Share"** or **"Send"** option in these apps, enabling you to send content via email, social media, or other communication apps.

## Shortcuts and Automation

Siri Shortcuts and automation through the Shortcuts app allow you to streamline tasks and routines on your iPhone 15 Pro Max, making it more efficient and personalized.

Access Shortcuts App: Open the **"Shortcuts"** app on your iPhone. If you don't see it on your home screen, you can find it in the App Library or by searching.

Create a Shortcut: Tap the **"+"** button in the upper right corner to create a custom Siri Shortcut. You'll enter the Shortcut creation screen.

Add Actions: Tap the **"Add Action"** button to select actions from various categories. These actions will be performed when you trigger the Shortcut.

Configure Actions: After adding actions, you can customize their settings by tapping them. For example, you can set a specific message for a **"Send Message"** action.

Name Your Shortcut: Tap **"Next"** to name your Shortcut. This name will be used to trigger Siri.

Add to Siri: Tap **"Add to Siri"** to record a phrase you'll tell Siri to trigger the Shortcut. Once registered, you can use that phrase to activate the Shortcut with your voice.

Finish and Test: Tap **"Done"** to finish creating the Shortcut. You can test it by saying the Siri phrase you recorded.

✓ Automating Tasks with the Shortcuts App:

Open the Shortcuts App: Launch the **"Shortcuts"** app.

Create or Edit a Shortcut: You can create or edit a new Shortcut or an existing one.

Add Automation: Tap the automation icon (a crescent moon) at the bottom of the screen.

Create Automation: Tap the **"+"** button to create a new automation.

Choose a Trigger: Select a trigger that will start your automation. For example, "Time of Day" or "Arrive Home."

Configure Trigger Details: Set up the specifics of the trigger. For example, if you chose "Time of Day," select the time.

Add Actions: After defining the trigger, tap **"Add Action"** to specify what actions the Shortcut should perform when the trigger occurs.

Finish and Enable: After setting up the automation, tap **"Next"** and review your settings. If everything looks correct, tap **"Done"** to enable the automation.

✓ Downloading and Managing Pre-Made Shortcuts:

Open the Shortcuts App: Launch the **"Shortcuts"** app.

Gallery: Tap the **"Gallery"** tab at the bottom of the screen. Here, you'll find a collection of pre-made Shortcuts created by others.

Browse and Download: Grasp the Shortcuts available in the Gallery. When you find one you like, tap it to view details and tap **"Add Shortcut"** to add it to your library.

Manage Shortcuts: To manage your Shortcuts, go to the **"My Shortcuts"** tab. You can organize, edit, and delete your custom and downloaded Shortcuts from here.

✓ Customizing Automation Based on Routines:

Create a Custom Shortcut: Use the Shortcuts app to create a custom Shortcut tailored to your routine. For example, you can create a "Morning Routine"

Shortcut that turns on specific lights, sets the thermostat, and plays your favorite morning playlist.

Set Up Automation: Once you've created your routine-specific Shortcut, follow the steps mentioned earlier to set up an automation trigger based on time, location, or other criteria that match your routine.

Customize Further: You can customize the Shortcut and automation to fit your needs and preferences.

## HomeKit and Smart Home Integration

With HomeKit and the Home app on your iPhone, you can easily manage and control your smart home devices, create custom scenes and automation, and even control your smart home remotely for added convenience and security.

Prepare Your Device: Make sure your HomeKit-compatible smart device is powered on and connected to the same Wi-Fi network as your iPhone 15 Pro Max.

Open the Home App: Open your iPhone's **"Home" app.** You may need to set up your home if it's your first use.

Add Accessory: Tap the **"+"** button in the upper right corner to add a new accessory. Select "Add Accessory."

Scan the QR Code or Enter Code Manually: Most HomeKit devices have a QR code. Scan it with your iPhone's camera. If not, you can enter the setup code manually.

Follow Setup Instructions: Follow the on-screen instructions provided by the device manufacturer; this typically involves connecting your device to the HomeKit ecosystem and giving it a name.

Assign to a Room: You can assign the device to a specific room in your home to help organize and control multiple devices more easily.

✓ Controlling Smart Home Accessories with the Home App:

Open the Home App: Launch the **"Home" app** on your iPhone 15 Pro Max.

View Your Accessories: You'll see a list of your HomeKit-compatible accessories. Tap on an accessory to control it. You can adjust settings, turn it on or off, and customize its behavior.

Use Voice Commands: If Siri is enabled, you can control your devices using voice commands. For example, say, "Hey, Siri, turn off the lights."

✓ Creating Scenes and Automation in HomeKit:

Scenes: Scenes are predefined settings for multiple accessories. To create a scene, go to the Home app, tap the **"+"** button, and select "Add Scene." Choose the accessories and settings you want to include and name your scene.

Automation: Automation allows you to set up triggers and conditions for your accessories. For example, you can create an automation that turns on the lights when you arrive home. To create an automation, go to the Home app, tap **"Automation,"** and follow the prompts to set up your trigger, conditions, and actions.

✓ Managing HomeKit Devices Remotely:

Home Hub: To remotely control HomeKit devices (outside your home Wi-Fi network), you need a Home Hub; this can be an iPad, Apple TV, or HomePod that stays at home and acts as a bridge.

Enable Remote Access: On your Home Hub device, go to **"Settings" > "Home" > "[Your Home]" > "Allow Remote Access;"** this allows you to control your HomeKit devices using the Home app even when you're not on the same Wi-Fi network.

Secure Your Home Hub: Make sure your Home Hub is updated and securely configured to protect your smart home.

# Augmented Reality (AR) and ARKit

Augmented Reality on your iPhone 15 Pro Max opens up a platform of immersive gaming, navigation, learning, and creativity.

App Store: Open the App Store on your iPhone.

Search for AR Apps: Use the search bar and enter keywords like "augmented reality," "AR games," or "AR experiences" to find a variety of AR apps.

Browse Categories: Notice the **"Apps"** tab in the App Store and look for categories like "AR Games," "AR Navigation," and "AR Education."

Read Reviews and Descriptions: Before downloading, read user reviews and app descriptions to get an idea of the AR experience offered by each app.

Download: Once you find an AR app that interests you, tap "Get" to download it. Open the app and follow the on-screen instructions to use AR content.

✓ Using AR Apps for Gaming, Navigation, and Learning:

AR Gaming: AR games like Pokémon GO and Minecraft Earth let you interact with virtual objects and characters in the real world using your iPhone's camera. Download AR games from the App Store and follow in-game instructions.

AR Navigation: Apps like Google or Apple Maps offer AR navigation features that overlay directions onto the natural world through your iPhone's camera. Open the navigation app and look for AR options.

AR Learning: Educational apps like AR Anatomy and Star Walk provide interactive and informative AR experiences. Search for educational AR apps in the App Store and learn various topics.

✓ Developing AR Apps with ARKit (for Developers):

Xcode: If a developer wants to create AR apps, you'll need Xcode, Apple's integrated development environment (IDE).

ARKit: ARKit is Apple's framework for building augmented reality experiences. Familiarize yourself with ARKit's documentation and resources on the Apple Developer website.

Swift: Learn Swift, Apple's programming language, as it's commonly used for developing iOS and AR apps.

Tutorials and Courses: Take advantage of online tutorials and courses focused on AR development with ARKit. There are many resources available, including video tutorials and written guides.

Test on Real Devices: Use a physical iPhone 15 Pro Max or ARKit-compatible device for testing and development. Xcode provides tools for deploying apps to your device.

✓ Configuring AR Preferences and Settings:

Access AR Settings: Open your iPhone's **"Settings"** app.

Privacy: For privacy settings related to AR apps, go to **"Privacy" > "Camera."** Here, you can see which apps have requested access to your camera for AR purposes and grant or revoke access as needed.

ARKit Apps: Some AR apps may have settings within the app. Check the app's settings for options related to AR features, such as graphics quality and permissions.

## Find My iPhone and Lost Mode

Find My is a tool for locating and securing your lost or stolen iPhone.

Enable Find My iPhone: To activate Find My iPhone on your iPhone 15 Pro Max, go to **"Settings" > [your name] > "Find My" > "Find My iPhone."** Turn on the **"Find My iPhone"** toggle.

Sign In to iCloud: Ensure you're signed in with your Apple ID. You can do this in **"Settings" > [your name] > "iCloud."**

Locate Your Device: If your iPhone is lost or stolen, you can use another Apple device with Find My iPhone or visit the iCloud website (icloud.com/find) on a computer to locate it. Sign in with your Apple ID, and you'll see your device's location on a map.

✓ Locating a Lost or Stolen Device:

Open Find My: Use the Find My app on another Apple device or visit iCloud.com/find on a computer.

Sign In: Sign in with your Apple ID.

View Device Location: The map will show your device's last location. You can use features like **"Play Sound"** to make your iPhone emit a loud sound if it's nearby.

✓ Enabling Lost Mode for Added Security:

Activate Lost Mode: Select your lost iPhone from the list of devices in the Find My app or on the iCloud website.

Enable Lost Mode: Tap **"Lost Mode"** (or "Activate" on the website); this locks your device, prevents unauthorized access, and allows you to display a custom message on the lock screen.

Set a Passcode: You can set a passcode for your device if it doesn't already have one. This passcode will be required to unlock the device.

Contact Information: Add contact information (like a phone number) to the lost device's lock screen message.

Turn on Notifications: Enable notifications to receive updates on your device's location.

Complete Activation: Confirm the activation of Lost Mode.

✓ Remote Wiping and Locking of the Device:

Activate Lost Mode: Follow the above steps to activate Lost Mode for your lost device.

Erase Your Device: If you believe your device is lost for good or are concerned about your data falling into the wrong hands, you can remotely erase it. Select your device in the Find My app or on the iCloud website, and then tap **"Erase This Device."** Confirm the action. Note that erasing the device will delete all data, so use this option cautiously.

Report to Authorities: If your device has been stolen, consider reporting the theft to the local authorities. They may be able to help you recover it.

## Siri and Voice Commands

Customizing Siri's voice and behavior allows you to tailor your virtual assistant to your preferences and make your interactions with Siri more personalized and efficient.

Activate Siri: You can activate Siri by saying **"Hey Siri"** followed by your command or by pressing and holding the side button on your iPhone 15 Pro Max.

Natural Language: Siri understands natural language, so you can ask questions or conversationally give commands. For example, you can say, "Hey Siri, what's the weather like today?" or "Hey Siri, set a timer for 10 minutes."

Multitasking: Siri can handle multitasking commands. For instance, say, "Send a message to John and set a timer for 5 minutes."

Follow-up Questions: Siri can handle follow-up questions based on the context of your previous query. For example, after asking about the weather, you can say, "What about tomorrow?"

✓ Using Siri for Device Control and Information:

Device Control: Siri can control various functions on your iPhone, such as turning on/off Wi-Fi and Bluetooth, adjusting screen brightness, or opening specific apps. For example, say, "Hey Siri, turn on Wi-Fi" or "Hey Siri, open the Messages app."

Information Retrieval: You can ask Siri to provide information like the weather forecast, sports scores, stock prices, or definitions. For example, "Hey Siri, what's the latest news?" or "Hey Siri, define 'serendipity.'"

Reminders and Calendar: Siri can set reminders and calendar events. Say, "Hey Siri, remind me to buy groceries tomorrow at 3 PM," or "Hey Siri, schedule a meeting for Friday at 2 PM."

Navigation: Use Siri for navigation by saying, "Hey Siri, give me directions to [destination]." Siri will open the Maps app and provide directions.

✓ Creating Personalized Siri Shortcuts:

Open the Shortcuts App: Launch the **"Shortcuts"** app on your iPhone 15 Pro Max.

Create a New Shortcut: Tap the **"+"** button in the upper right corner to create a new Shortcut.

Add Actions: Tap **"Add Action"** to select the actions you want the Shortcut to perform. You can choose from a wide range of measures available.

Customize and Name Your Shortcut: Configure the actions and customize the Shortcut as needed. Please give it a name.

Add to Siri: Tap **"Add to Siri"** to record a phrase that will trigger the Shortcut when you say it to Siri.

Test Your Shortcut: After creating the Shortcut, test it by saying the trigger phrase to Siri.

✓ Customizing Siri's Voice and Behavior:

Change Siri's Voice: To change Siri's voice, go to **"Settings" > "Siri & Search" > "Siri Voice."** Here, you can select a different Siri voice.

Customize Siri Responses: In "Settings" > "Siri & Search," you can configure how Siri responds to your requests. You can choose to have Siri speak responses or provide them silently.

Language and Region: You can change Siri's language and region preferences in the Siri settings; this is useful if you speak multiple languages or are in a different region.

# CHAPTER FIVE

# Understanding Accessibility Features

Accessibility ensures that technology is usable and beneficial for everyone, regardless of their abilities or disabilities. It's vital because it promotes inclusivity and equal access to information and services.

Apple recognizes the significance of accessibility and has integrated numerous features into its devices, including the iPhone 15 Pro Max, to support users with various needs.

✓ Accessing Accessibility Settings on the iPhone:

Open Settings: Unlock your iPhone and go to the home screen.

Access Settings: Tap the **"Settings"** app, represented by a gear icon.

Accessibility: Scroll down and tap **"Accessibility;"** this is where you can find and configure a wide range of accessibility features.

## VoiceOver and Screen Reader Options

VoiceOver is a screen reader that reads the screen's contents aloud and allows users with visual impairments to navigate the device.

✓ Enabling VoiceOver for Audio Feedback:

Open Settings: Navigate to your iPhone 15 Pro Max home screen and tap the **"Settings"** app.

Accessibility: Scroll down and tap **"Accessibility."**

VoiceOver: In the Accessibility settings, tap **"VoiceOver."**

Enable VoiceOver: Toggle the switch at the top of the VoiceOver screen to enable it. When VoiceOver is on, your iPhone will provide spoken feedback for on-screen elements.

✓ Navigating the Interface with VoiceOver:

Once VoiceOver is enabled, you can navigate the interface using gestures and voice commands:

Single Tap: Tap once to select an item.

Double Tap: Double-tap to activate or open the selected item.

Flick Right or Left: Swipe right or left with one finger to move through items on the screen.

Swipe Up or Down: Swipe up or down with one finger to scroll through content, like webpages or lists.

Control by Touch: Drag your finger around the screen to switch the layout and locate items. VoiceOver will announce the item under your finger.

Two-Finger Tap: Use a two-finger double-tap to perform the equivalent of a single tap on the screen.

Three-Finger Swipe Right or Left: Swipe right or left with three fingers to move between pages or screens.

Three-Finger Tap: A three-finger single-tap is often used to toggle VoiceOver on and off quickly.

✓ Customizing VoiceOver Settings:

VoiceOver Settings: In the VoiceOver settings (found in "Accessibility" > "VoiceOver"), you'll find various options to customize VoiceOver to your preferences.

Speech: Under "Speech," you can adjust the speaking rate, voice, and verbosity to make VoiceOver speak more quickly or slowly and provide more or less information.

Braille: If you use a Braille display, you can configure Braille settings to work with VoiceOver.

Audio: Customize audio settings, such as the sound of VoiceOver feedback.

Rotor: The Rotor is a customizable tool that allows you to perform various actions like adjusting the speaking rate, moving between headings, and more. You can set up the Rotor in the VoiceOver settings.

✓ Other Screen Reader Options:

Apart from VoiceOver, built into iOS, you can visit other screen reader options available in the App Store. Some popular third-party screen readers for iOS include:

Voice Dream Reader: This app is known for its versatility in reading various types of content, including documents, eBooks, web articles, and more.

JAWS (for Windows): If you use a Windows computer, JAWS (Job Access With Speech) is a widely used screen reader.

## Magnifier and Zoom

The Magnifier and Zoom features on your iPhone 15 Pro Max provide valuable visual assistance for low-vision users or those needing to zoom in on specific details.

Enable Magnifier: To enable the Magnifier, open the **"Settings"** app on your iPhone.

Accessibility: Scroll down and tap **"Accessibility."**

Magnifier: Tap **"Magnifier."**

Enable Magnifier: Toggle the switch at the top of the Magnifier settings screen to enable it.

Triple-Click Shortcut (Optional): You can assign a triple-click shortcut for quickly launching the Magnifier. Scroll down and choose "Accessibility Shortcut." Select "Magnifier."

Launch Magnifier: To use the Magnifier, triple-click your iPhone's side button (or home button, if applicable). Alternatively, you can open it from the Control Center by swiping down from the upper-right corner and tapping the Magnifier icon.

Zoom In and Adjust: Use the slider or pinch-to-zoom gestures to magnify the area you want to view. You can also use the flashlight to illuminate objects in low-light situations.

Freeze and Capture: Tap the shutter button to freeze the image temporarily. You can then adjust the zoom level and use the capture button to save the image if needed.

✓ Enabling and Configuring Zoom:

Enable Zoom: To enable the system-wide Zoom feature on your iPhone 15 Pro Max, open the "Settings" app.

Accessibility: Scroll down and tap "Accessibility."

Zoom: Tap "Zoom."

Enable Zoom: Toggle the switch at the top of the Zoom settings screen to enable it.

Zoom In and Out: Once Zoom is enabled, you can double-tap the screen with three fingers to zoom in and out. Alternatively, you can use a three-finger pinch gesture to adjust the zoom level.

Zoom Controller: You can also use the Zoom Controller, which provides on-screen buttons for zooming and panning. Customize the controller's appearance and behavior in the Zoom settings.

Zoom Region: In the Zoom settings, you can choose between "Full Screen Zoom" and **"Window Zoom."** Full-Screen Zoom magnifies the entire screen, while Window Zoom provides a movable and resizable zoomed-in window.

Smart Typing: If you enable Smart Typing in the Zoom settings, your keyboard will automatically adjust when using Zoom to ensure the text field remains visible.

Zoom Filter: Customize the appearance of the Zoom filter to enhance contrast or invert colors for better visibility.

✓ Managing Zoom Preferences and Shortcuts:

Zoom Preferences: You can customize Zoom further by adjusting preferences like maximum zoom level, minimum zoom level, and more. These options are available in the Zoom settings.

Zoom Shortcuts: To quickly access Zoom without going into settings, you can assign a shortcut. Go to **"Settings" > "Accessibility" > "Accessibility Shortcut"** and choose "Zoom." Now, you can triple-click the side button to activate Zoom.

# Display and Text Size Options

Adjusting text size, style, and other display settings helps to make your device more comfortable and tailored to your preferences.

Text Size: To adjust text size on your iPhone, open the **"Settings"** app.

Display & Text Size: Scroll down and tap **"Display & Text Size."**

Text Size: Under "Text Size," use the slider to make text larger or smaller. As you adjust the slider, you'll see a preview of the text size on the screen.

Bold Text: You can also enable **"Bold Text"** from the same screen to make text throughout the system appear in a bold font for increased readability.

Larger Accessibility Sizes: If the default text size isn't large enough, tap "Larger Accessibility Sizes" at the bottom to access more granular text size adjustments.

Dynamic Type: Some apps support Dynamic Type, allowing you to set a preferred text size within the app. To adjust this, go to **"Settings" > "Accessibility" > "Display & Text Size" > "Larger Text,"** then toggle on "Larger Accessibility Sizes." Open the app and look for text size settings within its preferences.

✓ Enabling Bold Text and Dark Mode:

Bold Text: To enable Bold Text for system-wide use, go to "Settings" > "Display & Text Size" and toggle on "Bold Text." Your device will restart to apply the changes.

Dark Mode: To enable Dark Mode for a darker interface and reduced eye strain in low-light conditions, go to **"Settings" > "Display & Brightness."** Under the **"Appearance"** section, choose "Dark." You can also set it to "Light" or "Auto" to automatically activate Dark Mode in the evening.

✓ Configuring Color Filters and Tint:

Color Filters: If you need to adjust the colors on your screen for better visibility, go to "Settings" > "Accessibility."

Display & Text Size: Tap "Display & Text Size."

Color Filters: Under "Color Filters," toggle the switch to enable them.

Filter Options: You can select various color filter options based on your needs. For example, you can choose Grayscale, Red/Green Filter, or Blue/Yellow Filter.

Intensity: Adjust the intensity of the selected color filter by using the slider.

✓ Using Smart Invert for Dark Mode in Apps:

Smart Invert: To enable a form of "dark mode" within apps that don't natively support it, go to "Settings" > "Accessibility."

Display & Text Size: Tap "Display & Text Size."

Smart Invert: Under "Color Filters," you'll find "Smart Invert Colors." Toggle this switch to enable it.

Effect: Smart Invert inverts the colors on the screen but does so intelligently to avoid inverting images and media. It creates a dark mode-like experience in apps that use primarily white backgrounds.

## AssistiveTouch and Gesture Controls

AssistiveTouch and gesture controls are potent tools for users who may have difficulty with traditional touch gestures or button presses.

Open Settings: Launch the "Settings" app on your iPhone 15 Pro Max.

Accessibility: Scroll down and tap **"Accessibility."**

Touch: Under the "Touch" section, tap **"AssistiveTouch."**

Enable AssistiveTouch: Toggle the switch at the top of the AssistiveTouch settings screen to enable it.

✓ Customizing On-Screen Controls:

Custom Actions: In the AssistiveTouch settings, you can configure custom actions for various on-screen controls. Tap "**Customize Top Level Menu**" to edit the menu items.

Add Actions: Tap the "**+**" button to add a new action. You can choose from some actions, including device, system, and accessibility functions.

Reorder Actions: To rearrange menu items, tap and hold the three-line icon next to an action, then drag it to the desired position.

Remove Actions: To remove an action, swipe left on it and tap "Delete."

Reset: To revert to the default menu, tap "Reset" at the bottom of the Customize Menu screen.

Using Gesture Controls and Shortcuts:

AssistiveTouch allows you to perform various gestures and shortcuts using on-screen controls:

Single Tap: Tap the AssistiveTouch button to perform a single tap at the current location.

Double Tap: Double-tap the AssistiveTouch button for a double-tap action.

Long Press: Press the AssistiveTouch button to simulate a long press.

Custom Gestures: You can also create and save custom gestures. To do this, go to "Settings" > "Accessibility" > "Touch" > "AssistiveTouch" > "Create New Gesture." Follow the on-screen instructions to record your custom gesture.

Configuring Touch Accommodations:

Touch Accommodations: Under the AssistiveTouch settings, you'll find "Touch Accommodations." Tap this option to access settings that help with touch sensitivity and interaction.

Hold Duration: You can adjust the duration required for a touch and hold gesture. Longer durations may be more comfortable for some users.

Ignore Repeat: Toggle this switch to prevent the device from registering multiple taps when you hold your finger on the screen.

Touch Accommodations Menu: This menu provides shortcuts to touch-related settings, such as Hold Duration, Ignore Repeat and Tap Assistance. You can quickly access and adjust these settings here.

## Hearing Accessibility Features

The hearing accessibility features on your iPhone are designed to enhance your auditory experience, provide alerts for essential sounds, and make communication more accessible for users with hearing impairments.

Open Settings: Launch the "Settings" app on your iPhone 15 Pro Max.

Accessibility: Scroll down and tap "Accessibility."

Sound Recognition: Under the "Hearing" section, tap "Sound Recognition."

Enable Sound Recognition: Toggle the switch at the top of the Sound Recognition settings screen to enable it.

Sounds: You can select specific sounds for recognition, such as sirens, dogs barking, doorbells, and more. Tap "Sounds" to choose the ones you want your device to alert you.

Notifications: Under "Notifications," you can choose how you want to be notified when a recognized sound is detected. Options include a notification banner, a notification sound, and haptic feedback.

✓ Configuring Headphone and Audio Settings:

Headphone Accommodations: To enhance audio for headphones, go to "Settings" > "Accessibility."

Audio/Visual: Scroll down and tap "Audio/Visual."

Headphone Accommodations: Under "MFi Hearing Devices," tap "Headphone Accommodations."

Enable Headphone Accommodations: Toggle the switch at the top of the screen to enable this feature.

Customize Audio Settings: You can adjust audio settings such as Audio Customization, Transparency Mode, and Headphone Safety. Customize these settings based on your hearing preferences.

✓ Using Live Listen with Compatible Hearing Devices:

Live Listen: If you have compatible hearing devices like AirPods, you can use Live Listen to boost the audio from your surroundings.

Connect Hearing Devices: Ensure your hearing devices are connected to your iPhone. Then, go to "Settings" > "Accessibility."

Hearing Devices: Under the "Hearing" section, tap "Hearing Devices."

Live Listen: Toggle on "Live Listen" to enable the feature.

Select Hearing Device: If you have multiple hearing devices paired, select the one you want to use with Live Listen.

Adjust Volume: Use the volume slider to control the amplification level of the audio from your hearing device.

✓ Customizing Vibration and Audio Notifications:

Sound and Haptics: You can customize vibration and audio notifications for calls, texts, and other events.

Open Settings: Go to "Settings" > "Sounds & Haptics."

Customize Notifications: Under "Sounds and Vibration Patterns," tap on specific notification types (e.g., Ringtone, Text Tone) to select different sounds or vibrations.

Vibration Patterns: You can create custom vibration patterns by tapping "Vibration" and selecting "Create New Vibration."

## Visual Accessibility Features

Visual accommodations and adjustments are designed to make the iPhone more accessible and comfortable for users with specific visual needs or preferences.

Open Settings: Launch the "Settings" app on your iPhone 15 Pro Max.

Accessibility: Scroll down and tap "Accessibility."

Display & Text Size: You'll find various visual accommodations options under the "Display & Text Size" section.

Invert Colors: You can toggle on "Smart Invert" to reverse colors, making the display easier on the eyes in low-light situations. For more specific color adjustments, choose "Color Filters" and select a filter that suits your needs.

Auto-Brightness: **Enable "Auto-Brightness"** to allow your iPhone to adjust screen brightness based on ambient lighting conditions automatically.

Reduce White Point: This option allows you to reduce the intensity of bright colors on the screen. Adjust the slider to your preferred level.

✓ Using Display Accommodations for Color Adjustments:

Color Filters: To access color adjustment settings, go to "Settings" > "Accessibility."

Display & Text Size: Under "Display & Text Size," tap "Color Filters."

Enable Color Filters: Toggle on "Color Filters" to activate this feature.

Choose a Filter: Select a color filter that best suits your needs. Options include Grayscale, Red/Green Filter, Blue/Yellow Filter, and more.

Intensity: Adjust the intensity of the selected color filter using the slider.

✓ Reducing Motion and Transparency Effects:

Reduce Motion: To minimize motion effects on your iPhone, go to "Settings" > "Accessibility."

Motion: Under "Motion," toggle on "Reduce Motion;" this will reduce animations and parallax effects.

Increase Contrast: To enhance visual clarity, enable "Increase Contrast" in the same "Accessibility" menu; this will reduce transparency effects and increase the contrast of UI elements.

✓ Customizing the Screen Curtain:

The Screen Curtain is a feature that turns off the screen when activated, making it useful for those who rely on VoiceOver or auditory feedback. Here's how to use it:

Activate Screen Curtain: To turn on the Screen Curtain, triple-tap with three fingers on the screen when VoiceOver is enabled.

Deactivate Screen Curtain: Triple-tap with three fingers again to turn off the Screen Curtain.

## Speech and Interaction

Speech and interaction features on the iPhone are designed to provide alternative communication and control methods for users who may have difficulty with traditional touch or voice commands.

Open Settings: Launch the "Settings" app on your iPhone 15 Pro Max.

Accessibility: Scroll down and tap "Accessibility."

Spoken Content: You'll find options for spoken feedback under the "Spoken Content" section.

Speak Selection: Toggle on "Speak Selection" to enable it. This feature allows your iPhone to read selected text out loud.

Speak Screen: Toggle on "Speak Screen" to enable it. With this feature, you can swipe down from the top of the screen with two fingers to have the entire screen's content read aloud.

Highlight Content: You can highlight content as it's spoken by toggling on "Highlight Content" under the Speak Screen settings.

✓ Configuring Voice Control for Device Control:

Voice Control: Voice Control is a powerful feature that allows you to control your device using voice commands. To enable it, go to "Settings" > "Accessibility."

Voice Control: Under the "Touch" section, tap "Voice Control."

Enable Voice Control: Toggle on "Voice Control."

Customize Commands: You can customize voice commands to perform various actions on your device. Discover the available commands and create your custom commands.

✓ Using Type to Siri for Text Input:

Type to Siri: Type to Siri allows you to interact with Siri by typing text instead of voice commands. To enable it, go to "Settings" > "Accessibility."

Siri: Under the "Siri" section, tap "Type to Siri."

Enable Type to Siri: Toggle on "Type to Siri."

Interact with Siri: Now, when you activate Siri, you can type your requests, and Siri will respond accordingly.

✓ Customizing Spoken Content Preferences:

Spoken Content Preferences: To configure how said content is presented, return to the "Spoken Content" settings under "Accessibility."

Speech: You can customize spoken content's speaking rate, voice, and pronunciation.

Highlight Words: Enable "Highlight Words" if you want the text to be visually highlighted as it's spoken.

Typing Feedback: You can also enable "Typing Feedback," which provides spoken feedback as you type on the keyboard.

# Switch Control and External Devices

Switch Control is an accessibility feature that allows individuals with motor impairments to control their iPhones using external switches or adaptive devices.

Open Settings: Launch the "Settings" app on your iPhone 15 Pro Max.

Accessibility: Scroll down and tap **"Accessibility."**

Switch Control: Under the "Touch" section, tap **"Switch Control."**

Enable Switch Control: Toggle on "Switch Control" at the top of the settings screen.

Add a Switch: To use external switches or devices, tap **"Switches."** You can add a control by selecting a source (e.g., Camera, Screen, External) and configuring the switch's behavior.

Customize Scanning Style: Switch Control uses scanning to navigate on-screen elements. You can customize the scanning style by tapping "Scanning

Style" and choosing from Auto or Manual Scanning options.

Adjust Scanning Settings: Under **"Scanning Settings,"** you can configure scanning options, including scanning speed, audio cues, and more.

Use Switch Control: With Switch Control enabled and switches configured, you can interact with your iPhone by activating the buttons according to your setup. Scanning will highlight items on the screen, and you can select an item by activating a switch.

✓ Connecting External Accessibility Devices:

To connect external accessibility devices like specialized switches, head pointers, or communication devices, you may need specific hardware adapters or Bluetooth connectivity. The process can vary depending on the device you're using. Refer to the manufacturer's instructions or consult with an assistive technology specialist for guidance on connecting your specific device to your iPhone 15 Pro Max.

✓ Switch Recipes and Configurations:

Switch Control allows you to create and customize switch recipes, actions triggered by specific switch activations. To navigate switch recipes and configurations:

In the "Switch Control" settings, tap **"Switch Recipes."**

You can create, edit, or delete switch recipes based on your needs. These recipes define what happens when you activate switches.

Configure actions for each switch state (e.g., single press, double press) within a recipe. You can set actions like navigation, selection, or system functions.

Customize the timing and order of actions within a switch recipe to suit your preferences.

✓ Compatibility with Assistive Devices:

Switch Control is designed to work with many assistive devices, including switches, joysticks, and head pointers. The compatibility of these devices may depend on their specific features and communication methods, such as USB, Bluetooth, or wireless connectivity.

Ensure that your external assistive device is compatible with iOS 17 and that you have any necessary adapters or drivers to connect it to your iPhone 15 Pro Max. Consider seeking assistance from an assistive technology specialist or Apple's Accessibility Support for guidance on setting up and configuring external accessibility devices with Switch Control.

# CHAPTER SIX

## Setting Up iCloud

Setting up iCloud and managing your iCloud storage is necessary for ensuring your data is securely backed up and accessible across your Apple devices.

Open Settings: Launch the **"Settings"** app on your iPhone 15 Pro Max.

Your Apple ID: Tap your Apple ID profile at the top of the Settings menu. Your Apple ID should display your name and profile picture if you have one.

iCloud: In the Apple ID menu, you'll see "iCloud" listed as an option. Tap **"iCloud"** to access iCloud settings.

✓ Logging in with Your Apple ID:

Sign In: If you haven't already signed in with your Apple ID, you'll see a "Sign in to your iPhone" prompt at the top of the iCloud settings screen. Tap it.

Enter Apple ID: Enter your Apple ID and password in the respective fields. If you enable two-factor authentication, you may need to enter a verification code sent to your trusted devices.

Sign In: Tap "Sign In" to complete the login process.

✓ Reviewing and Managing iCloud Storage:

Manage Storage: In the iCloud settings, you can tap "Manage Storage" to review and manage your iCloud storage.

Storage Breakdown: You'll see a breakdown of how your iCloud storage is being used, including which apps and data are taking up space.

Backups: You can manage your device backups, including deleting old backups or selecting which apps to back up.

Photos: You can review your iCloud Photos settings, including whether you want to optimize iPhone storage or keep full-resolution images on your device.

Messages: If you use iCloud for Messages, you can manage your message storage settings.

Other Apps: You may also see different apps and services that use iCloud for data storage. You can manage these settings here.

✓ Free and Paid Storage Options:

iCloud offers both free and paid storage options. Here's a brief overview:

Free Storage: Every Apple ID is allocated 5 GB of free iCloud storage. This storage is shared across all your Apple devices and accounts associated with that Apple ID.

Paid Storage Plans: You can subscribe to paid storage plans if you need more storage. These plans offer additional storage space, starting from 50 GB and going up to 2 TB.

Upgrade Storage: To upgrade your storage plan, tap **"Manage Storage"** in the iCloud settings and then **"Change Storage Plan."** Follow the on-screen instructions to select and purchase a plan that suits your needs.

Shared Storage: You can also share your iCloud storage with family members by setting up Family Sharing. Each family member can have their own Apple ID but share the storage plan.

Storage Management: To efficiently manage your iCloud storage, regularly review which apps and data use the most space, delete unnecessary backups, and consider optimizing your photo storage settings.

## Enabling iCloud Backup

Enabling iCloud Backup ensures your iPhone's data is regularly and securely backed up. Automatic backups occur daily when your device meets the required conditions (Wi-Fi, charging, and locked). You can also initiate manual backups whenever you want to ensure your data is up to date.

Open Settings: Launch the **"Settings"** app on your iPhone 15 Pro Max.

Your Apple ID: Tap your Apple ID profile at the top of the Settings menu.

iCloud: In the Apple ID menu, tap **"iCloud."**

iCloud Backup: Scroll down and tap **"iCloud Backup."**

Enable iCloud Backup: Toggle "iCloud Backup" to turn automatic backups on. Your device will back up to iCloud when connected to Wi-Fi, plugged in, and locked.

✓ Initiating a Manual iCloud Backup:

You can manually initiate an iCloud backup at any time if you want to back up immediately:

iCloud Backup: In the "iCloud Backup" settings **(Settings > [Your Apple ID] > iCloud > iCloud Backup)**, you'll see a **"Back Up Now"** option. Tap it.

Wait for Backup: Your iPhone will start the manual backup process; this may take some time, depending on how much data is backed up.

Check Backup Status: You can check the progress of the backup on the same screen. Ensure your device is connected to Wi-Fi and has sufficient battery or is plugged in to complete the backup.

✓ Managing and Viewing Backup Contents:

You can control and view the contents of your iCloud backup:

iCloud Backup Settings: To see what's being backed up, go to the "iCloud Backup" settings (**Settings > [Your Apple ID] > iCloud > iCloud Backup**). You'll see a list of apps and data categories included in the backup.

App Data: Some apps may allow you to manage their data individually. For example, you can manage your WhatsApp chat backups in the WhatsApp app settings.

✓ Checking the Last Backup Date and Time:

To see the date and time of your last iCloud backup:

iCloud Backup Settings: In the **"iCloud Backup"** settings (Settings > [Your Apple ID] > iCloud > iCloud Backup), you'll find the date and time of the last successful backup under **"Back Up Now."**

Storage Management: You can also check the last backup date and time in iCloud settings' **"Manage Storage"** section. Tap "Manage Storage," then select your device from the list to view backup details.

## Restoring from an iCloud Backup

Restoring from an iCloud backup helps you recover your data and settings after a device reset or when setting up a new iPhone.

1. Erase All Content and Settings: If you want to restore your iPhone 15 Pro Max from an iCloud backup, you'll first need to erase all content and settings on the device to make way for the restoration.

Go to **"Settings" > "General" > "Reset."**

Choose **"Erase All Content and Settings."**

Confirm the action by entering your passcode or Apple ID credentials.

2. Start the Setup Process: After erasing, your iPhone will restart, and you'll be greeted with the initial setup screen.

3. Setup Assistant: Follow the on-screen instructions until you reach the **"Apps & Data"** screen.

4. Restore from iCloud Backup: Choose **"Restore from iCloud Backup"** on the "Apps & Data" screen.

5. Sign in to iCloud: Sign in with your Apple ID and password associated with the iCloud backup you want to restore from.

6. Select Backup: Choose the iCloud backup you want to restore from. The list will display the date and time of each backup.

7. Restore: The restoration process will begin. Your device will download and restore your apps, data, and settings from the chosen backup.

✓ Restoring Specific App Data from iCloud:

1. If you want to restore specific app data from iCloud (e.g., WhatsApp chats or Health data):

2. Apps with Individual Restores: Some apps, like WhatsApp, allow you to restore their data individually from within the app's settings. Open the

app and navigate to its backup/restore settings to initiate the process.

3. Health Data: Health data can be restored along with the overall device restore. Ensure that **"Health"** is enabled in the list of apps when you choose an iCloud backup for restoration.

✓ Setting Up Your Device After a Restore:

1. After the restoration is complete, you'll need to finish setting up your device:

2. On-Screen Prompts: Complete the setup process by following the on-screen prompts; this includes setting up your Apple ID, passcode, Face ID, and other preferences.

3. Apps: Your apps will be reinstalled from the App Store, and their data will be restored from the iCloud backup.

4. Messages: Your iMessage and SMS messages should be restored as part of the iCloud backup.

5. Photos: If you use iCloud Photos, your photos and videos will download to your device.

6. Check Data: Ensure that all your data and settings are as expected.

✓ Troubleshooting:

If you encounter issues during the restoration process:

1. Stalled or Slow Restore: If the restore seems to take a long time, ensure you have a stable Wi-Fi connection and a sufficient battery charge.

2. Error Messages: If you receive error messages, note them, as they can help identify the issue. Common errors include insufficient space, connectivity problems, or issues with your Apple ID.

3. Check iCloud Storage: Ensure that you have enough iCloud storage space to accommodate the backup you're restoring from.

4. Update iOS: Make sure your iPhone 15 Pro Max is running the latest iOS 17 version, as outdated

software can sometimes cause issues during restoration.

5. Contact Apple Support: If you encounter persistent problems, consider contacting Apple Support for assistance.

## Managing iCloud Drive

iCloud Drive makes storing, organizing, and sharing files convenient across your Apple devices.

Storage: iCloud Drive provides storage space in the cloud, and the available storage capacity depends on your iCloud subscription plan.

Synchronization: Files stored in iCloud Drive are synchronized across all your Apple devices, including iPhone, iPad, Mac, and even Windows PCs (via iCloud for Windows).

Access: You can access your files stored in iCloud Drive from any device with your Apple ID and the iCloud Drive app or via the Files app on iOS and iPadOS devices.

✓ Accessing Files Stored in iCloud Drive:

To access files stored in iCloud Drive:

Files App: Open the **"Files"** app on your iPhone. This app provides access to all your files stored in iCloud Drive.

Browse Files: Browse and navigate through your files and folders, similar to a traditional file explorer.

Search: You can use the search bar at the top to quickly find specific files or folders.

Recent: The **"Recents"** tab shows files you've recently accessed or modified.

Tags: Files can be tagged to help you organize and find them more easily.

✓ Managing Folders and File Organization:

You can organize your files and folders in iCloud Drive:

Create Folders: To create a new folder, tap the **three dots** in the upper-right corner of the Files app, then choose **"New Folder."** Name your folder and select where to place it.

Move and Organize: You can drag and drop files and folders to rearrange or move them into other folders.

Delete Files: Swipe left on a file or folder and tap **"Delete"** to remove it. Deleted items are moved to the **"Recently Deleted"** folder before being permanently deleted.

Tagging: You can assign tags to files and folders to categorize and organize them better.

✓ Sharing Files with Others Using iCloud Drive:

You can easily share files stored in iCloud Drive with others:

Select File: In the Files app, tap the file you want to share.

Share: Tap the share button (a square with an upward arrow) at the top-right corner.

Choose a Sharing Method: You can send the file via Messages, Mail, AirDrop, or various third-party apps.

Set Permissions: Configure sharing permissions, such as view-only or edit access, and select recipients.

Share Link: You can also create a shareable link that allows others to access the file without needing an iCloud account.

Stop Sharing: You can stop sharing a file at any time by going to the shared file's details and selecting **"Stop Sharing."**

## Syncing Across Devices

Using iCloud to sync data across your Apple devices lets you enjoy a seamless and cohesive experience, ensuring that your contacts, calendars, photos, and more are always up-to-date and accessible from any of your devices.

iCloud Sign-In: Ensure that you are signed in with the same Apple ID on all your Apple devices, including iPhone, iPad, and Mac.

iCloud Settings: On each device, go to **"Settings"** (on iOS and iPadOS) or "System Preferences" (on macOS) and navigate to the "iCloud" settings.

Syncing Options: In the iCloud settings, you'll find various syncing options for data types, such as Contacts, Calendars, Reminders, Photos, and more.

Enable Sync: Toggle on the syncing options you want to enable. For example, turn on the **"Contacts"** toggle switch to sync Contacts. Repeat this for other types of data you want to sync.

Merge or Replace: When enabling syncing for the first time, you may be asked whether you want to merge your existing data or replace it with data from iCloud. Choose the option that suits your needs.

Wait for Sync: Your devices will now sync data with iCloud. This process may take some time, especially if you have significant data.

✓ Continuity Between iPhone, iPad, and Mac:

To ensure a smooth experience and continuity between your Apple devices, consider the following tips:

Use the Same Apple ID: Sign in with the same Apple ID on all your devices; this is essential for syncing data and maintaining a consistent experience.

Enable Handoff: Handoff allows you to start a task on one device and continue it on another. To enable Handoff, go to **"Settings" > "General" > "Handoff"** on iOS and iPadOS devices. On macOS, go to **"System Preferences" > "General"** and check **"Allow Handoff."**

iCloud Drive: It stores documents and files in the cloud, making them accessible from all your devices. Enable iCloud Drive in iCloud settings.

AirDrop: AirDrop lets you quickly share files between nearby Apple devices. Ensure AirDrop is enabled in Control Center (on iOS and iPadOS) or Finder (on macOS).

Universal Clipboard: If you're using devices with macOS Sierra (or later) and iPadOS 10 (or later), Universal Clipboard allows you to copy and paste content between devices. Ensure both Wi-Fi and Bluetooth are enabled.

✓ Syncing Contacts, Calendars, and Reminders:

To sync Contacts, Calendars, and Reminders between your Apple devices:

Go to "Settings" (on iOS and iPadOS) or "System Preferences" (on macOS).

Navigate to the "iCloud" settings.

Toggle on "Contacts," "Calendars," and "Reminders" to enable syncing for these items.

Your contacts, calendar events, and reminders will now be synced across your devices.

✓ Managing Synced Device Preferences:

You can manage device-specific preferences in each device's settings. For example, you can independently adjust notification preferences, display settings, and app-specific settings on each device.

# iCloud Photos and Videos

iCloud Photos is a feature that securely stores your entire photo and video library in iCloud; this makes your pictures and videos accessible from all your Apple devices.

Open Settings: Launch the **"Settings"** app on your iPhone 15 Pro Max.

Your Apple ID: Tap your Apple ID profile at the top of the Settings menu.

iCloud: In the Apple ID menu, tap **"iCloud."**

Photos: Scroll down and tap **"Photos."**

Enable iCloud Photos: Toggle on **"iCloud Photos."** You may see a message asking whether you want to download photos and videos to your device. Choose the option that suits your preference.

Optimize iPhone Storage: If you are low on 'device' storage, you can enable **"Optimize iPhone Storage."** This setting stores full-resolution photos and videos in iCloud and keeps smaller, optimized versions on your device.

✓ Accessing and Organizing Photos in iCloud:

Once iCloud Photos is enabled, you can access and organize your photos and videos:

Photos App: Open your iPhone's **"Photos"** app to view your entire photo library.

Organize Albums: You can organize your photos into albums, create new albums, and add pictures to them.

Search: Use the search bar to find specific photos or videos by keywords, locations, or dates.

Edit: You can edit photos and videos directly within the Photos app.

Delete: Deleting a photo or video from the Photos app removes it from iCloud if iCloud Photos is enabled.

✓ Managing iCloud Photos Settings:

You can customize iCloud Photos settings to suit your preferences:

Settings: In the "Photos" settings (**Settings > [Your Apple ID] > iCloud > Photos**), you'll find various options.

iCloud Photos: You can toggle "iCloud Photos" on or off anytime.

Download and Keep Originals: If you want to keep full-resolution copies of photos and videos on your device, enable **"Download and Keep Originals."**

My Photo Stream: If you prefer not to use iCloud Photos but still want to sync recent photos across your devices, you can enable **"My Photo Stream."**

✓ Photo and Video Sharing Options:

iCloud Photos offers various sharing options:

Shared Albums: You can create shared albums and invite friends and family to view and contribute photos and videos.

iCloud Photo Sharing: You can share individual photos or videos with others using iCloud Photo Sharing.

AirDrop: You can use AirDrop to share photos and videos with nearby Apple devices quickly.

Messages and Email: You can send photos and videos via messages or email directly from the Photos app.

Social Media: Easily share photos and videos on social media platforms like Facebook, Instagram, and X/Twitter.

Third-Party Apps: Many third-party apps support iCloud Photos integration, allowing you to access your photos and videos within those apps.

# iCloud Mail and Notes

iCloud Mail is Apple's email service that allows you to send, receive, and manage email using your Apple ID.

✓ Setting Up iCloud Mail:

Open Settings: Launch the **"Settings"** app on your iPhone.

Your Apple ID: Tap your Apple ID profile at the top of the Settings menu.

iCloud: In the Apple ID menu, tap **"iCloud."**

Mail: Scroll down and toggle on **"Mail"** to enable iCloud Mail.

Apple ID Verification: If prompted, verify your Apple ID by entering your password.

Mail App: Open the "Mail" app on your iPhone. You'll find your iCloud Mail account set up and ready to use.

✓ Syncing Notes Across Devices with iCloud:

iCloud also allows you to sync notes across all your Apple devices. Here's how to set it up:

Notes Sync:

Open Settings: Go to **"Settings"** on your iPhone.

Your Apple ID: Tap your Apple ID profile.

iCloud: Scroll down and toggle on **"Notes"** to enable syncing.

Accessing Notes: Open the "Notes" app to access and create notes that will sync across your devices.

✓ Managing Email and Notes in the iCloud Environment:

Once iCloud Mail and Notes are set up, you can control them on your iPhone, iPad, Mac, and even via **iCloud.com** (webmail). Here are some everyday tasks:

iCloud Mail:

Sending and Receiving Email: Use the Mail app to send and receive emails from your iCloud Mail account.

Organizing Email: You can create folders, move emails to different folders, mark emails as read or unread, and manage your email as you would with any email service.

iCloud Notes:

Creating Notes: Open the Notes app to create and edit notes. You can organize notes into folders and add images, links, and checklists.

Syncing Notes: Any notes you create or edit on one device will sync automatically with all your other Apple devices linked to the same iCloud account.

Sharing Notes: You can share notes by tapping the **"Share"** button in the Notes app and entering their email addresses or phone numbers.

✓ Troubleshooting Email and Notes Sync:

If you encounter synchronization issues with iCloud Mail or Notes:

Check Internet Connection: Ensure that your device is connected to the internet via Wi-Fi or cellular data.

Verify Apple ID: Ensure you are signed in with the correct Apple ID on all devices.

Toggle Sync Off and On: In iCloud settings (**Settings > [Your Apple ID] > iCloud**), you can try turning off iCloud Mail and Notes syncing, then turning it back on.

Update iOS 17: Ensure that your iPhone is running the latest version of iOS to benefit from bug fixes and improvements.

Contact Apple Support: If issues persist, consider contacting Apple Support for assistance.

# iCloud Keychain and Passwords

iCloud Keychain is a built-in feature that securely stores and manages your passwords, credit card information, and personal details, making it easy to autofill passwords and forms on your Apple devices.

✓ Setting Up iCloud Keychain:

Open Settings: Launch the **"Settings"** app on your iPhone 15 Pro Max.

Your Apple ID: Tap your Apple ID profile at the top of the Settings menu.

iCloud: In the Apple ID menu, tap **"iCloud."**

Keychain: Scroll down and toggle on **"Keychain"** to enable iCloud Keychain.

Apple ID Verification: If prompted, verify your Apple ID by entering your password.

✓ Storing and Auto-Filling Passwords:

Once iCloud Keychain is enabled, it can securely store and autofill your passwords across your Apple devices:

Password Autofill: When you're on a website or app that requires a login, iCloud Keychain will offer to autofill your saved passwords.

Password Generation: iCloud Keychain can also generate strong, unique passwords when you sign up for new accounts.

Security Code Autofill: For websites that use two-factor authentication with SMS codes, iCloud Keychain can autofill the code sent to your phone.

✓ Managing and Updating Saved Passwords:

You can control and update your saved passwords and other information:

Settings: In the **"Passwords & Accounts"** section of Settings, you can access and edit your saved passwords.

Edit Passwords: To edit a saved password, tap on it and select **"Edit."** You can change the password, username, or other details.

Remove Passwords: To delete a saved password, tap on it and choose "Delete Password."

AutoFill Passwords: In the "Passwords & Accounts" section, you can turn the AutoFill Passwords feature on or off.

## iCloud Family Sharing

Family Sharing allows you to share iCloud services with your family members, including iCloud storage and App Store purchases.

✓ Enabling Family Sharing:

Open Settings: Launch the **"Settings"** app on your iPhone 15 Pro Max.

Your Apple ID: Tap your Apple ID profile at the top of the Settings menu.

Family Sharing: In the Apple ID menu, tap **"Family Sharing."**

Set Up Your Family: Tap **"Get Started"** and follow the on-screen instructions to set up your family group. You can invite family members to join by sending invitations.

Invite Family Members: You can send invites via iMessage or create child accounts for family members under 13.

Choose Services to Share: After setting up your family group, you can choose which services to share, including iCloud storage, App Store purchases, Apple Music, and more.

✓ Sharing iCloud Storage and Purchases with Family Members:

Once Family Sharing is set up, you can share iCloud services and purchases with your family members:

iCloud Storage: To share iCloud storage, go to **"Settings" > "Family Sharing" > "iCloud Storage."** You can share a plan that suits your family's needs.

App Store Purchases: All purchases from family members can be shared, including apps, games, movies, music, and subscriptions.

Family Calendar: A shared family calendar helps you coordinate events and appointments.

Family Photo Album: Share photos and videos with your family members in a shared album.

Find My: Use the **"Find My"** app to locate family member's devices and share your location with them.

✓ Managing Family Accounts and Purchases:

As the organizer of the family group, you can manage family accounts and purchases:

Approve Purchases: You can set up **"Ask to Buy"** for child accounts, allowing you to approve or decline their app and media purchases.

Manage Family Members: You can add or remove family members, create child accounts, and manage their settings.

Payment Methods: You can set up a shared payment method for family purchases or allow family members to use their own.

Share Subscriptions: Family members can share subscriptions to Apple services like Apple Music and Apple TV+.

Family Sharing Settings: Customize Family Sharing settings to suit your family's needs, such as location sharing and shared calendars.

Sharing Purchases: All family members can access purchased content from the App Store, iTunes Store, and Apple Books. Go to the respective app and check the **"Purchased"** section.

## iCloud Storage and Data Management

Here's how to check and manage your iCloud storage usage:

✓ Checking iCloud Storage Usage:

Open Settings: Launch the **"Settings"** app on your iPhone 15 Pro Max.

Your Apple ID: Tap your Apple ID profile at the top of the Settings menu.

iCloud: In the Apple ID menu, tap **"iCloud."**

Manage Storage: Under the **"iCloud Storage"** section, tap "Manage Storage." Here, you'll see a breakdown of your storage usage.

✓ Upgrading iCloud Storage Plans:

If you're running low on iCloud storage, you can upgrade your plan:

Manage Storage: Follow the steps above to reach the "Manage Storage" screen.

Change Storage Plan: Tap **"Change Storage Plan."**

Choose a Plan: Select the storage plan that suits your needs and tap **"Buy"** to confirm the purchase.

Deleting and Managing Backups and Data:

To free up space in iCloud, consider deleting unnecessary backups and managing your data:

   ✓ Managing Backups:

Settings: Go to **"Settings"** > **[Your Apple ID]** > **"iCloud."**

Manage Storage: Under **"iCloud Storage,"** tap **"Backups."**

Select a Backup: Tap a backup to see its details.

Delete Backup: At the bottom, tap **"Delete Backup"** to remove the backup for a specific device.

   ✓ Managing Data:

Settings: In **"Settings,"** go to **"iCloud"** > **"Manage Storage."**

App Data: Tap on an app to see the data it's storing in iCloud. You can delete data for individual apps here.

Photos: To manage your photos and videos, go to **"Photos" > "Storage"** within the Photos app. Here, you can enable "Optimize iPhone Storage" to save space by storing lower-resolution versions on your device.

✓ Keeping iCloud Storage Organized:

To maintain an organized and efficient iCloud storage:

Regularly Review Data: Periodically review your stored data and delete items you no longer need.

Use Optimize iPhone Storage: Enable **"Optimize iPhone Storage"** in the Photos settings to save space on your device while keeping full-resolution photos in iCloud.

Backup Only What You Need: Be selective with what you back up. You can choose which apps and data are included in your iCloud backups.

Enable iCloud Desktop & Documents: On Mac, you can enable iCloud Desktop & Documents to store these files in iCloud and free up space on your Mac's hard drive.

Clean Up Old Backups: Review and delete old device backups you no longer use.

Monitor Storage: Keep an eye on your storage usage in **"Settings" > [Your Apple ID] > "iCloud" > "Manage Storage;"** this will help you identify and address storage-hungry items.

# CHAPTER SEVEN

# Downloading and Updating Apps

To help you navigate through downloading and updating apps on your iPhone 15 Pro Max, here are the steps:

✓ Accessing the App Store

Unlock Your iPhone: Begin by unlocking your iPhone 15 Pro Max. You can do this by either using Face ID or entering your passcode.

Find the App Store Icon: Look for the App Store icon on your home screen. It resembles a blue "A" made from a pencil, pen, and brush.

Tap the App Store Icon: Once you've located the icon, tap on it to open it.

✓ Browsing and Searching for Apps

Go through the App Store: Upon opening the App Store, you'll be on the "Today" tab, which features recommended apps. You can access several tabs at the bottom of the screen, such as "Apps," "Games," "Search," and more.

Browse Categories: Tap the "Apps" tab to discover apps by category. You can then select specific categories like "Health & Fitness," "Productivity," or "Entertainment."

Search for Apps: If you know the name of the app you want, tap on the "Search" tab at the bottom right corner. Enter the app's name in the search bar and tap **"Search."** Results will appear, and you can tap on the app you want to learn more about.

✓ Downloading and Installing Apps

Select an App: When you find an app you want to download, tap on its icon or name to open its detailed page.

Get or Install: On the app's page, you'll see a button that says either **"Get"** or **"Install."** Tap this button.

Face ID Confirmation: If prompted, use Face ID or enter your Apple ID password to confirm the download and installation.

Wait for Download: The app will begin downloading, and its icon will appear on your home screen once the download is complete.

✓ Updating Apps to the Latest Versions

App Store Updates: To update your apps, open the App Store.

Tap Your Profile: In the upper right corner of the App Store, tap on your profile picture or initials.

Scroll Down to Updates: Scroll down to the **"Available Updates"** section. Here, you'll see a list of apps with available updates.

Update All or Select Apps: You can tap **"Update All"** at the top or individually tap **"Update"** next to each app you want to update.

Confirmation: Confirm the updates with your Face ID or Apple ID password if prompted.

## Organizing Apps on the Home Screen

Organizing apps on the home screen of your iPhone gives a clutter-free and efficient user experience.

✓ Rearranging App Icons and Folders

Enter Editing Mode: To rearrange apps, lightly touch and hold any app icon or folder on the home screen until it jiggles. You'll also see an **"Edit Home Screen"** option at the top of the screen.

Drag and Drop: In editing mode, you can drag and drop app icons or folders anywhere on the home screen. Please place them in the desired order or move them to other pages by swiping left or right.

Create App Folders: Drag one app icon onto another to create a folder, creating a folder with both apps inside. You can rename the folder by tapping on its name.

Exit Editing Mode: When you're done rearranging, press the **"Done"** button in the upper right corner of the screen to exit editing mode. Your changes will be saved.

✓ Using the App Library

Access the App Library: The App Library is a convenient way to access and organize apps without cluttering your home screen. To access it, swipe left until you reach the last home screen page.

Search or Browse: You can search for specific apps in the search bar at the top or browse apps by category in the App Library. Tap on any app to open it.

Add Apps to Home Screen: If you want to add an app from the App Library to your home screen, tap and hold the app icon, then drag it to the home screen.

✓ Deleting Apps and Offloading Unused Ones

Enter Editing Mode: To delete apps, enter editing mode by lightly touching and holding an app icon until it starts jiggling.

Delete Apps: Tap the **"X"** icon in the corner of the app you want to delete. Confirm the deletion when prompted.

Offload Unused Apps: To automatically offload apps you rarely use, go to **Settings > General > [Your**

**Name] > iCloud** and enable **"Offload Unused Apps;"** this will remove apps you don't use frequently but keep their data.

Reinstall Offloaded Apps: If you ever need an offloaded app, you can easily reinstall it from the App Store.

**Note:** Some pre-installed apps cannot be deleted but can be hidden from the home screen if you don't use them.

## Managing App Permissions

Managing app permissions on your iPhone ensures your privacy and security.

App Permissions Overview: When you install an app, it may request access to various device features and data, such as location, camera, microphone, contacts, photos, etc. These are known as app permissions.

Purpose of Permissions: App permissions are necessary for apps to function correctly. For example, a map app needs access to your location to provide navigation.

✓ Granting and Revoking App Permissions

Accessing App Permissions: Go to **Settings > Privacy** on your iPhone to manage app permissions.

Location Services: Go to **Settings > Privacy > Location Services** to grant or revoke location access. Here, you can toggle location access for individual apps.

Camera and Microphone: You can manage camera and microphone access under **Settings > Privacy > Camera** and **Settings > Privacy > Microphone,** respectively.

Other Permissions: For additional permissions like contacts, photos, and more, navigate to the corresponding sections under Settings > Privacy.

✓ Privacy Considerations

Limit Access: Only grant permissions to apps with a legitimate need. For instance, a photo editing app should have access to your photos, but a game may not need such access.

Check App Settings: Some apps offer in-app settings to customize permissions further. Check within the app for these options.

App Store Descriptions: Review app descriptions on the App Store to understand why specific permissions are needed; this can help you make informed choices when downloading apps.

App Tracking Transparency: It prompts you to allow or deny apps from tracking your activity across other apps and websites. Consider your privacy preferences when responding to these prompts.

Privacy Nutrition Labels: Some apps provide "privacy nutrition labels" on the App Store, detailing what data they collect and how it's used. Pay attention to these labels when choosing apps.

✓ Revoking Permissions

Regularly Review Permissions: Review the permissions granted to apps in your settings. If you no longer use an app or believe it doesn't need a particular permission, revoke it.

App Updates: Be aware that updating an app may reset its permissions. After updating, check and adjust permissions as needed.

## Using Essential Built-in Apps

Utilizing the essential built-in apps on your iPhone 15 Pro Max is a great way to enhance your productivity and organization.

✓ Pre-Installed Apps

Home Screen: You'll find various pre-installed apps on your iPhone's home screen. Some of these are essential for daily tasks and organization.

App Library: You can also access these apps by swiping left on the home screen to reach the App

Library; this is a convenient way to find and organize apps.

✓ Using Notes

Creating a Note:

Open Notes: Tap the **"Notes"** app icon on your home screen or in the App Library.

Create a New Note: Tap the **"+"** button in the bottom left corner to create a new note.

Add Content: Type, paste, or dictate text into your note. You can also insert images, sketches, checklists, and links.

Formatting: Use the formatting options at the top to change text style and add bullets, numbers, or titles.

Organizing Notes:

Folders: You can organize your notes into folders. To create a folder, tap **"Edit"** in the top left corner of the main Notes screen, then tap **"New Folder."**

Move Notes: To move a note into a folder, tap **"Edit"** in the note view, then select the folder to which you want to move it.

✓ Using Calendar

Creating Events:

Open Calendar: Tap the **"Calendar"** app icon on your home screen or in the App Library.

Create an Event: Tap the **"+"** button at the bottom center to create a new event.

Add Details: Enter event details like the title, location, date, and time.

Set Alerts: You can set event reminders by tapping **"Add Alert."**

Viewing and Managing Events:

Day/Week/Month View: Switch between views to see your events.

Edit or Delete: Tap on an event to edit or delete it.

✓ Using Reminders

Creating Reminders:

Tap the **"Reminders"** app icon on your home screen or in the App Library.

Create a Reminder: Tap the **"+"** button at the bottom left to create a new reminder.

Add Details: Enter the reminder's title, date, and time if needed.

Set Priorities: You can assign priorities (high, medium, or low) to your reminders.

Organizing Reminders:

Lists: You can create lists to group related reminders. Tap **"Add List"** to create one.

Move Reminders: To move a reminder to a different list, tap and hold it, then drag it to the desired list.

Completed Reminders: When you complete a reminder, tap the circle next to it to mark it as done.

# Multitasking and App Switching

Multitasking and switching between open apps on your iPhone aids in a smooth user experience.

✓ Switching Between Open Apps

Home Gesture: You can switch between open apps using gestures. To switch to a recently used app, swipe left or right along the screen's bottom edge. This gesture replaces the home button's double-click action.

Switching Method: Swipe to the right to go to the previously used app, and swipe to the left to return to the current app or switch to the next one. You can continue swiping to navigate through multiple open apps.

✓ Accessing the App Switcher

Gesture Shortcut: To access the App Switcher, swipe up from the bottom edge of the screen and pause for a moment (about halfway up the screen). This gesture will reveal the App Switcher, displaying all your recently used apps in a card-like view.

Navigation: You can see all the open apps in the App Switcher. Swipe left or right to scroll through them horizontally.

✓ Closing Apps to Save Battery Life

While it's generally not necessary to manually close apps on iOS since the system manages them efficiently, there are situations where you might want to close an app to save battery life or troubleshoot issues.

✓ Manually Closing Apps

Access the App Switcher: Use the earlier gesture to access the App Switcher.

Swipe Up to Close: In the App Switcher, swipe up on the app card you want to close. Swipe it to the top of the screen to force close the app.

✓ When to Close Apps

Battery Saving: Closing apps can help conserve battery life if you notice that a particular app consumes more power than expected.

App Not Responding: If an app becomes unresponsive or freezes, closing and reopening it can resolve the issue.

Privacy Concerns: Closing an app can prevent it from running in the background and potentially accessing your data when unnecessary.

Note: iOS 17 is designed to manage apps efficiently and suspends background processes for most apps when they are not in use. Closing apps should be done selectively when necessary rather than as a routine practice.

## Notifications and Alerts

Managing notifications and alerts on your iPhone 15 Pro Max helps to stay informed without being

✓ Configure App Notifications

Access Notification Settings: Go to **Settings >
Notifications** on your iPhone.

Select an App: Scroll through the list of installed
apps and select the app for which you want to
configure notifications.

Enable or Disable Notifications: Toggle on or off the
**"Allow Notifications"** switch at the top to turn
notifications for that app on or off.

Customize Alert Style: Choose the type of
notification alert under "Alert Style When Unlocked."
You can choose banners, alerts, or none.

Notification Sounds: To change the sound for this
app's notifications, tap "Sound" and select a
different tone.

✓ Managing Notification Preferences

Notification Grouping: You can group notifications
by app or keep them separate. Toggle on or off
**"Notification Grouping"** based on your preference.

Lock Screen: Under "Show Previews," choose whether notifications will be shown "Always," "When Unlocked," or "Never" on the lock screen.

Notification Center: Decide whether you want notifications from this app to appear in the Notification Center by toggling "Show in History" on or off.

✓ Handling App Notifications on the lock Screen

Interactive Notifications: When you receive a notification on the lock screen, you can interact with it without unlocking your device. Swipe left on a notice to reveal actions like **"Reply"** for messages or **"Clear"** to dismiss them.

Unlock to Open: If you want to unlock your device and open the app directly from the lock screen notification, swipe right on the notification.

✓ Managing App Badges and Sounds

App Badges: To manage app badges (the red notification numbers on app icons), go to **Settings >**

**Notifications** and select the app. Toggle on or off the **"Badge App Icon."**

Notification Sounds: To change the notification sound for all apps, go to **Settings > Sounds & Haptics.** You can customize the default sound for various types of notifications here.

App-Specific Sounds: To change the sound for a specific app's notifications, follow the "Configuring App Notifications" steps mentioned earlier.

## In-App Purchases and Subscriptions

Understanding and managing in-app purchases (IAPs) and subscriptions allows for responsible app usage on your iPhone.

### *What Are IAPs?*

In-app purchases are transactions made within apps to unlock premium content, features, or virtual goods. These can include extra lives in a game, ad-free experiences, or premium subscriptions.

## Types of IAPs

IAPs can vary widely. They may be one-time purchases, consumables (used once, like virtual currency), or subscriptions (ongoing access).

✓ Making Purchases Within Apps

Open the App: Launch the app from which you want to make an in-app purchase.

Access the Store: Look for an option like "Store," "Shop," or a shopping cart icon within the app.

Select the Item: Browse the available items or subscriptions and select the one you want to purchase.

Confirm Payment: You'll usually be prompted to confirm your purchase. You may need to enter your Apple ID password or use Face ID to authenticate the purchase.

Complete the Purchase: Once you confirm the payment, the item or subscription will be added to your account.

✓ Managing and Canceling Subscriptions

Access Subscriptions: Go to **Settings > [Your Name] > Subscriptions** on your iPhone 15 Pro Max to manage your subscriptions.

View Subscriptions: You'll see a list of your active subscriptions. Tap on one to view details.

Modify or Cancel: You can modify subscription options or cancel a subscription by selecting the appropriate options.

✓ Protecting Against Accidental Purchases

Use Screen Time: Consider using Screen Time to set up app purchase limits and restrictions, especially if you share your device with others.

Enable Ask to Buy (Family Sharing): If you use Family Sharing, enable "Ask to Buy" for children's accounts; this requires parental approval for app purchases.

Require Authentication: In **Settings > [Your Name] > iTunes & App Store,** you can configure when your Apple ID should require authentication for purchases, such as "Always Require" or "After 15 Minutes."

Password or Face ID: Ensure that your Apple ID requires a password or Face ID for purchases.

Review Purchases: Regularly review your purchase history in the App Store (under your Apple ID) to catch any unauthorized or accidental purchases.

## App Store Preferences and Restrictions

Configuring App Store preferences and restrictions, including setting up Family Sharing, enabling parental controls and Screen Time, and managing app downloads and content, helps to control and customize your app experience on your iPhone 15 Pro Max.

✓ Setting Up Family Sharing for App Purchases

Family Sharing Setup: To set up Family Sharing, go to **Settings > [Your Name] > Family Sharing** on your iPhone.

Invite Family Members: Tap **"Add Family Member"** and follow the prompts to invite family members to join your Family Sharing group.

Sharing App Purchases: With Family Sharing enabled, you can share app purchases. When you buy an app, it can be downloaded and used by family members without additional charges.

✓ Enabling Parental Controls and Screen Time

Parental Controls: Go to **Settings > Screen Time** to enable parental controls.

Turn on Screen Time: Tap **"Turn On Screen Time"** if it's not enabled. Follow the setup process.

Downtime: You can set specific downtime hours when only essential apps are accessible.

App Limits: Set daily time limits for app categories, including the App Store.

Content & Privacy Restrictions: Under Screen Time, tap **"Content & Privacy Restrictions"** to further customize restrictions for apps and content.

✓ Restricting App Downloads and Content

Content & Privacy Restrictions: Under Screen Time, as mentioned above, you can restrict app downloads by enabling restrictions for the App Store.

Restricting Content: You can also determine content based on age ratings. Under **"Content Restrictions,"** adjust apps, websites, and more settings.

✓ Configuring App Store Settings

App Store Settings: Go to **Settings > iTunes & App Store** to configure App Store settings.

Password Settings: Here, you can control when your Apple ID password is required for purchases.

Cellular Data: Manage whether app downloads and updates are allowed over cellular data or Wi-Fi only.

Automatic Downloads: Choose whether to automatically download purchased apps to other devices connected to your Apple ID.

Offload Unused Apps: Enable **"Offload Unused Apps"** to save storage by automatically removing apps you rarely use.

App Updates: Toggle on or off **"App Updates"** to automatically update apps when new versions are available.

# CHAPTER EIGHT

# Adjusting Display and Sound Settings

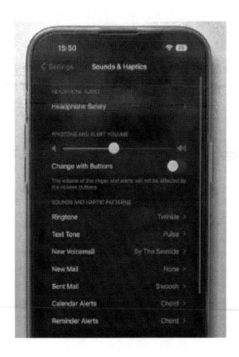

Adjusting display and sound settings can enhance your user experience and tailor it to your preferences.

✓ Changing Screen Brightness and Auto-Brightness

Access Display & Brightness: Go to **Settings >
Display & Brightness** on your iPhone 15 Pro Max.

Brightness: Use the slider to adjust the screen
brightness to your desired level.

Auto-Brightness: Toggle on or off **"Auto-Brightness"**
to allow your iPhone to adjust the screen brightness
based on ambient light conditions automatically.

✓ Adjusting Screen Timeout and Auto-Lock
  Settings

Access Display & Brightness: Go to **Settings >
Display & Brightness** on your iPhone.

Auto-Lock: Tap "Auto-Lock" to set the time for your
iPhone to lock the screen when not in use
automatically. Options range from 30 seconds to 5
minutes or "Never."

✓ Configuring Sound and Vibration Settings

Access Sound & Haptics: Go to **Settings > Sounds &
Haptics** on your iPhone.

Action Switch: You can press and hold the physical switch on the side of your iPhone to enable silent mode (mute all sounds) or ring mode (allow sounds).

Vibrate on Ring/Silent: Toggle on or off **"Vibrate on Ring"** and "Vibrate on Silent" to turn on or off vibration for incoming calls and alerts.

- ✓ Customizing Ringtone and Notification Sounds

Access Sounds & Haptics: Go to **Settings > Sounds & Haptics** on your iPhone.

Ringtone: Tap **"Ringtone"** to choose a custom ringtone from the list. You can also purchase or download additional ringtones from the iTunes Store.

Text Tone: Customize your text message notification sound by tapping **"Text Tone."**

New Mail, Sent Mail, etc.: You can also set unique notification sounds for notifications (e.g., new mail, sent mail, calendar alerts) within the **"Sounds & Haptics"** settings.

# Configuring Privacy and Security

Configuring privacy and security settings on your iPhone protects your personal information and ensures your device's security.

✓ Setting Up Face ID or Passcode

Access Face ID & Passcode Settings: Go to **Settings > Face ID & Passcode** on your iPhone.

Set Up Face ID: If your iPhone supports Face ID, tap **"Enroll Face"** and follow the on-screen instructions to set up Face ID; this will enable facial recognition for unlocking your device and authorizing secure actions.

Set Up a Passcode: If you prefer using a passcode, tap **"Turn Passcode On"** and follow the prompts to create a passcode. This passcode will serve as an alternative or backup to Face ID.

✓ Enabling Two-Factor Authentication (2FA)

Access Password & Security: Go to **Settings > [Your Name] > Password & Security** on your iPhone.

Enable Two-Factor Authentication: Tap **"Two-Factor Authentication"** and follow the on-screen instructions to set up 2FA for your Apple ID; this adds an extra layer of security to your account.

✓ Managing App Permissions and Privacy Settings

Access App Privacy Settings: Go to **Settings > Privacy** on your iPhone.

Manage App Permissions: Here, you can view and control app permissions for location, camera, microphone, contacts, photos, and more. Tap each category to see which apps have access and adjust their permissions.

✓ Reviewing Location Services and Privacy Controls

Access Location Services: Go to **Settings > Privacy > Location Services** on your iPhone.

Review App Permissions: Here, you'll see a list of apps with location access. You can individually customize location permissions for each app.

Location Sharing: If you share your location with friends or family, you can manage those settings by tapping **"Share My Location."**

System Services: Under **"Location Services,"** tap **"System Services"** to review and control system-level location settings.

## Managing Battery and Storage

Efficiently managing battery and storage on your iPhone enables a smooth user experience.

✓ Checking Battery Health and Usage Statistics

Access Battery Settings: Go to **Settings > Battery** on your iPhone.

Battery Health: Under **"Battery Health,"** you can check your battery's maximum capacity and whether it needs to be replaced. If it's significantly degraded, you'll see a recommendation for service.

Battery Usage: Scroll down to view battery usage by apps; this provides insights into which apps consume the most battery.

✓ Optimizing Battery Life and Power-Saving Tips

Low Power Mode: Enable It by going to **Settings > Battery** and toggling it; this reduces background activity and extends battery life.

Background App Refresh: Under **Settings > General > Background App Refresh,** you can turn off this feature for specific apps or altogether.

Location Services: Go to **Settings > Privacy > Location Services** to review and limit app location access.

Screen Brightness: Lower screen brightness in **Settings > Display & Brightness** and consider enabling Auto-Brightness.

Auto-Lock: Shorten the Auto-Lock timer in **Settings > Display & Brightness > Auto-Lock.**

Push Email: Fetch email less frequently. Go to **Settings > Mail > Accounts > Fetch New Data** to adjust the fetch settings.

App Updates: Enable automatic app updates in **Settings > App Store** so your apps stay up to date with efficiency improvements.

Managing Storage Space and Cleaning Up Unused Files

Access iPhone Storage: Go to **Settings > General > [Device] Storage** on your iPhone to see a breakdown of storage usage.

Offload Unused Apps: Enable **"Offload Unused Apps"** in **Settings > App Store** to automatically remove apps you rarely use while keeping their data.

Delete Unwanted Apps: Manually delete apps you no longer need by tapping on them and selecting **"Delete App."**

Review and Delete Photos: Go to the Photos app and review and delete any photos or videos you no longer want.

Messages and Attachments: In the Messages app, delete old conversations or remove message attachments by tapping **"Details"** in a conversation and selecting **"Manage."**

Safari Data: In **Settings > Safari,** you can clear browsing history, cookies, and website data.

Optimize Photos: Enable "Optimize iPhone Storage" in **Settings > Photos** to store high-resolution photos and videos in iCloud while keeping smaller versions on your device.

## Language and Region Settings

Access Language & Region Settings: Go to **Settings > General > Language & Region** on your iPhone 15 Pro Max.

Change Language: Under **"iPhone Language,"** tap **"Edit"** and select your preferred language from the list. You'll need to confirm your selection.

Change Region: To change the region, tap **"Region"** and select your desired area; this may affect the date and time format, currency, and other regional settings.

✓ Customizing Keyboard Layouts and Dictionaries

Access Keyboard Settings: Go to **Settings > General > Keyboard** on your iPhone.

Add Keyboards: Tap **"Keyboards"** to add new keyboard layouts. You can add multiple languages and switch between them while typing.

Customize Keyboards: Tap on a specific keyboard to customize its settings, including auto-correction, predictive text, and shortcuts.

Manage Dictionaries: Under **"Text Replacement,"** you can create custom text shortcuts for frequently used phrases.

✓ Using Multilingual Keyboard Support

Enable Multilingual Typing: If you've added multiple keyboards, you can enable **"Allow Full Access"** under **Settings > General > Keyboard > Keyboards** to switch between them while typing.

Switch Keyboards: Tap the globe or emoji icon on the keyboard to cycle through the available keyboards.

✓ Managing Regional Date and Time Settings

Access Date & Time Settings: Go to **Settings > General > Date & Time** on your iPhone.

Set Date and Time Automatically: Toggle **"Set Automatically"** to let your iPhone automatically update the date and time based on your current location.

Time Zone: You can manually select your time zone if needed. Toggle on **"24-Hour Time"** to use a 24-hour clock format.

Date Formats: Customize date and time formats under **"Date & Time Formats."**

## Network and Connectivity Settings

Configuring network and connectivity settings on your iPhone 15 Pro Max allows you to stay connected and manage your data usage effectively.

Access Wi-Fi Settings: Go to **Settings > Wi-Fi** on your iPhone.

Connect to a Wi-Fi Network: Tap the Wi-Fi network you want to connect to and enter the password if required.

Access Bluetooth Settings: Go to **Settings >
Bluetooth** to manage Bluetooth connections.
Toggle Bluetooth on or off and pair it with devices.

✓ Setting Up a Personal Hotspot

Access Personal Hotspot Settings: Go to **Settings >
Personal Hotspot** on your iPhone.

Enable Personal Hotspot: Toggle on **"Personal
Hotspot."** You can set a Wi-Fi password if desired.

Connect Devices: Other devices can connect to
your iPhone's hotspot by selecting it in their Wi-Fi
settings and entering the password.

✓ Managing VPN and Proxy Settings

Access VPN Settings: Go to **Settings > VPN** on your
iPhone.

Add VPN Configuration: Tap **"Add VPN
Configuration"** to set up a VPN connection. You'll
need to enter the details provided by your VPN
provider.

Proxy Settings: If needed, configure proxy settings for your Wi-Fi network. Go to **Settings > Wi-Fi,** tap the connected network, and scroll down to **"HTTP Proxy."**

✓ Reviewing Cellular and Data Usage

Access Cellular Data Settings: Go to **Settings > Cellular** on your iPhone.

Cellular Data Usage: Here, you can view your cellular data usage by app. Please scroll down to see a list of apps and their consumed data.

Cellular Data Options: In this section, you can manage your cellular data plan, enable or disable cellular data for specific apps, and reset data usage statistics.

Wi-Fi Assist: Under "Wi-Fi Assist," you can turn on or off the feature that automatically uses cellular data when Wi-Fi connectivity is poor.

## App-specific Settings

Access App Settings: Open the **"Settings"** app on your iPhone.

Scroll Down: Scroll down to find a list of installed apps. Tap the app for which you want to configure settings.

Customize App Settings: Within each app's settings, you can usually customize preferences related to that specific app. These settings vary widely depending on the app's features.

✓ Customizing App-Specific Preferences

App Preferences: Look for options like **"Preferences," "Settings,"** or **"Options"** within the app itself. Many apps allow you to customize various features, such as notification preferences, account settings, and display preferences.

In-App Settings: Sometimes, app-specific settings are accessed directly from within the app. Open the app, tap on your profile or account icon, and navigate the settings menu within the app.

✓ Managing App Notifications and Permissions

Access Notification Settings: Go to **Settings > Notifications** on your iPhone.

Select App: Scroll through the list of installed apps and select the app for which you want to configure notifications.

Customize Notifications: You can enable or remove notifications, choose notification styles, and customize alert tones for each app in its notification settings.

Manage App Permissions: For more granular control over app permissions (e.g., location, camera, microphone), go to Settings > Privacy and select the appropriate category (e.g., Location Services). Here, you can manage permissions for all apps.

✓ Resetting App Settings If Needed

Reset App Settings: If you encounter issues with an app or want to reset its settings to default, go to **Settings > General > Reset.**

Reset All Settings: You can choose **"Reset All Settings"** to reset all app settings to their defaults. Note that this will also reset other system settings.

## System and Software Updates

Keeping your iPhone 15 Pro Max up to date with the latest software enables security, performance, and access to new features.

✓ Checking for and Installing iOS Updates

Access Software Update: Go to your iPhone's **Settings > General > Software Update.**

Check for Updates: Tap **"Download and Install"** for available updates. If an update is available, follow the on-screen instructions to download and install it.

Install Later: If you prefer to install the update at a later time, tap **"Later"** and choose between **"Install Now"** or **"Remind Me Later."**

✓ Configuring Automatic Updates

Access Software Update Settings: Go to **Settings > General > Software Update.**

Configure Automatic Updates: Tap **"Customize Automatic Updates."** You can toggle on **"Download iOS updates"** and "Install iOS updates" to enable automatic updates.

✓ Managing Software Updates and Version Information

View iOS Version Information: Go to **Settings > General > About.** Here, you can see information about your device, including the iOS version.

Update iOS Over the Air: You can update your iOS version by going to **Settings > General > Software Update.**

Manage Downloaded Updates: If an update has been downloaded but not installed, you can manage it in **Settings > General > iPhone Storage.** Please tap on the update to delete it or install it.

Update via iTunes/Finder: You can update your iPhone by connecting it to a computer with iTunes (on macOS Catalina or earlier) or Finder (on macOS Catalina and later).

# CHAPTER NINE

## Taking Photos and Videos

Taking photos and videos with your iPhone 15 Pro Max is a fundamental feature. The Camera app icon looks like a camera and is usually on the home screen. Tap it to open the Camera app.

✓ Capturing Photos with the Rear and Front Cameras

Switch Between Rear and Front Cameras: In the Camera app, you can switch between the rear (primary) and front (selfie) cameras by tapping the camera switch icon, which typically looks like two arrows forming a circle. It's usually located at the screen's top right or top left corner.

Focus and Take a Photo: To focus, tap on the screen where you want the camera to focus. Then, tap the white shutter button (circle) to capture a photo. You can also use the volume buttons on the side of the phone as a shutter button.

✓ Recording Videos in Different Modes

Switch to Video Mode: In the Camera app, swipe the mode selector to the left or right until you reach the video mode. You can usually choose between different video recording modes like "Video," "Slow Motion," or "Time-Lapse."

Start Recording: To start recording, tap the red record button. To stop recording, tap the same button again.

Switch Between Video Modes: If you're using a specific video mode (e.g., Slow Motion), you can switch back to the standard video mode by swiping to the left or right in the mode selector.

✓ Using Burst Mode

Activate Burst Mode: Hold the shutter button (circle) while taking a photo in the Camera app. The iPhone will capture a series of pictures in rapid succession.

Select the Best Shot: After taking a burst of photos, go to the Photos app, find the burst photos you took, and tap on them. You can select the best shot from the burst; the rest will be stored in a separate burst album.

# Camera Modes and Features

The different camera modes and features on your iPhone 15 Pro Max can significantly enhance your photography experience.

✓ Camera Modes

Open the Camera App: Tap the Camera app icon on your iPhone's home screen.

Access Camera Modes: In the Camera app, swipe left or right on the screen to switch between different camera modes. Standard modes include Photo, Portrait, Action, Panorama, and more. Some methods are accessible via the "More" button.

Select a Mode: Tap on the mode you want to use. Each mode has its specific features and settings.

✓ Using the Timer and Exposure Adjustment

Access Timer: In the Camera app, tap the clock icon (timer) at the top of the screen. You can set a timer for 3 or 10 seconds before taking the photo.

Adjust Exposure: Tap on the screen where you want to set the focus and exposure. A yellow box with a sun icon will appear. Slide your finger up or down on the sun icon to adjust exposure manually.

✓ Grid and Level Features for Better Composition

Access Grid and Level: Go to **Settings > Camera** on your iPhone.

Enable Grid: Toggle on "Grid" to overlay a grid on the camera viewfinder; this helps with alignment and composition.

Enable Level: Toggle on "Level" to use a leveling tool that helps you keep your shots straight and avoid tilted horizons.

✓ Enabling HDR (High Dynamic Range)

Access HDR Settings: In the Camera app, tap the HDR icon at the top of the screen. It's usually represented by "HDR" or "Auto."

Select HDR Mode: You can choose "HDR Off," "HDR Auto," or "HDR On." "Auto" lets the camera decide when to use HDR based on lighting conditions, while "On" forces HDR mode for every shot.

## Editing Photos and Videos

Editing photos and videos is a valuable skill to enhance your multimedia creations.

Access Photos: Tap the "Photos" app icon on your iPhone's home screen to open it.

✓ Basic Photo Editing (Cropping, Rotating)

Select a Photo: Open the Photos app and select the photo you want to edit.

Access Edit Mode: Tap **"Edit"** at the top right corner of the screen.

Cropping: Tip the crop icon (a square with arrows) to crop the photo. Drag the corners or edges of the frame to adjust the crop area. Tap "Done" when you're satisfied.

Rotating: Tip the rotate icon (a circular arrow) to turn the photo. You can spin the image clockwise or counterclockwise. Tap "Done" when it's oriented correctly.

✓ Enhancing Photos with Filters and Adjustments

Select a Photo: Open the Photos app and choose the photo you want to enhance.

Access Edit Mode: Tap "Edit" at the top right corner of the screen.

Filters: Tap the filter icon (three overlapping circles) to apply various preset filters to your photo. You can adjust the intensity of the filter using the slider.

Adjustments: Tap the adjustments icon (dial) to fine-tune your photo. Here, you can adjust brightness, contrast, saturation, and more. Swipe left or right on the slider to make adjustments.

Save Changes: Tap "Done" when satisfied with the enhancements.

✓ Trimming and Editing Videos

Access Videos: Open the Photos app and select the video you want to edit.

Access Edit Mode: Tap "Edit" at the bottom of the screen when viewing the video.

Trimming: Drag the start and end handles on the timeline to trim the video. You can preview the trimmed video by tapping the play button.

Additional Editing: To perform more advanced video editing, you may want to use third-party video editing apps available on the App Store.

Save Changes: Tap "Done" to save your edited video.

## Organizing and Managing Photos

Organizing and managing photos helps you keep your memories in order and declutter your gallery.

✓ Creating Albums and Folders

Access the Photos App: Open your iPhone's "Photos" app.

Create an Album: Tap the "Albums" tab at the bottom of the screen. Then, tap the **"+"** icon at the top left corner and choose **"New Album."** Name the album and add photos to it.

Create a Folder: Tap the "Albums" tab, then tap **"See All"** next to "My Albums." Tap the "+" icon and select "New Folder." Name the folder and drag albums into it.

✓ Sorting and Organizing Photos

Access Albums: Open the "Photos" app and tap the "Albums" tab.

Drag and Drop: To rearrange photos within an album or move them between albums, tap "See All" next to an album and use drag-and-drop to reorganize.

✓ Deleting and Recovering Photos

Select Photos to Delete: In the "Photos" app, navigate to the album or view where the photos you want to delete are located.

Delete Photos: Tap "Select" at the top right corner, select the photos, and tap the trash can icon. Confirm the deletion.

Recover Deleted Photos: If you accidentally deleted photos, go to the "Albums" tab, scroll down to "Other Albums," and find the "Recently Deleted" album. Tap it, select the photos you want to recover, and tap "Recover."

✓ Using the Recently Deleted Folder

Access the Recently Deleted Folder: Open the "Photos" app, go to the "Albums" tab, and scroll down to "Other Albums." Tap "Recently Deleted."

Recover or Permanently Delete: Inside the Recently Deleted folder, you can select photos and videos to recover or tap "Delete All" to delete everything in the folder permanently.

## Sharing and Exporting Photos

Sharing and exporting photos is expected, whether you want to send them to friends, post on social media, or back them up to a computer or cloud storage.

✓ Sharing Photos via Messages and Social Media

Open Photos App: Launch the "Photos" app on your iPhone 15 Pro Max.

Select a Photo: Tap the photo you want to share.

Share Button: Tap the share button, represented by a square with an upward-pointing arrow. It's usually located at the bottom left corner of the screen.

Choose an App: Select the messaging or social media app you want to share the photo. For example, you can choose Messages, WhatsApp, Facebook, or Instagram.

App-specific Steps: Depending on the app you choose, follow the on-screen instructions to send the photo. You may need to select recipients, add a caption, or choose the privacy settings.

✓ Sending Photos via Email

Open Photos App: Launch the "Photos" app on your iPhone.

Select a Photo: Tap the photo you want to send via email.

Share Button: Tap the share button (square with an upward-pointing arrow).

Choose Mail: Select the "Mail" app from the sharing options.

Compose Email: Fill in the recipient's email address, subject, and any message you want to include. You can also choose the photo size by tapping "Small," "Medium," or "Large" just below the photo.

Send: Tap the "Send" button to send the email with the attached photo.

✓ Using AirDrop to Share with Nearby Devices

Access Control Center: Swipe down from the top right corner of your iPhone's screen to open Control Center.

Activate AirDrop: Long-press the network settings card (with Wi-Fi, Bluetooth, etc.), then tap "AirDrop." Select "Contacts Only" or "Everyone," depending on who you want to share with.

Select Photo: Open the "Photos" app, choose a photo, and tap the share button.

Choose AirDrop: Tap "AirDrop" and select the nearby device you want to share the photo with.

Accept on Receiving Device: The recipient's device will receive a notification asking if they want to accept the photo. Once they accept, the picture will be sent.

✓ Exporting Photos to a Computer or Cloud Storage

Connect to a Computer: Use your Type-C cable to connect your iPhone to a computer (Mac or PC).

Open File Explorer (Windows) or Finder (Mac): Your iPhone should appear as a device. Click on it to access your photos.

Select Photos: Navigate to the photos you want to export and copy/paste them to your computer.

Use iCloud or Cloud Storage Apps: You can also use iCloud or third-party cloud storage apps like Google Drive or Dropbox to sync and access your photos across devices. Install the app, sign in, and enable photo syncing.

## Live Photos and Effects

Live Photos and effects add a dynamic dimension to your iPhone 15 Pro Max photos.

✓ Viewing and Editing Live Photos

Open Photos App: Launch the "Photos" app on your iPhone.

Find a Live Photo: Scroll through your photos to locate a Live Photo (identified by a concentric ring icon at the top left).

View Live Photo: Tap the Live Photo to view it. Press and hold on to the photo to see it come to life with motion and sound.

Edit Live Photo: To edit a Live Photo, tap "Edit" at the top right corner while viewing it. You can apply filters, crop, adjust lighting, and more. Changes will apply to both the photo and the Live Photo portion.

✓ Using Live Photo Effects (e.g., Loop, Bounce)

Open Photos App: Launch the "Photos" app on your iPhone.

Select a Live Photo: Choose a Live Photo from your gallery.

Edit Live Photo: Tap "Edit" at the top right corner of the screen.

Effects: Swipe up on the Live Photo to reveal the "Effects" options. Here, you can choose from various properties like "Loop," "Bounce," or "Long Exposure."

Apply Effect: Tap the effect you want to apply. Preview it to see how it changes the Live Photo.

Save: Tap "Done" to save the edited Live Photo with the effect.

✓ Creating Long-Exposure Photos

Open Photos App: Launch the "Photos" app on your iPhone.

Select a Live Photo: Choose a Live Photo with the motion you want to turn into a Long Exposure shot.

Edil Live Pholo: Tap "Edit" at the top right corner of the screen.

Effects: Swipe up on the Live Photo to reveal the "Effects" options.

Choose Long Exposure: Select "Long Exposure."

Save: Tap "Done" to save the Long Exposure photo.

✓ Sharing Live Photos with Others

Open Photos App: Launch the "Photos" app on your iPhone.

Select a Live Photo: Choose the Live Photo you want to share.

Share Button: Tap the share button (square with an upward-pointing arrow) at the bottom left corner.

Choose Sharing Method: Select the sharing method, such as Messages, Mail, or social media apps.

Send or Share: Follow the on-screen instructions to send or share the Live Photo with others. Note that not all platforms support Live Photos, so they may sometimes be shared as regular photos or videos.

## Using Action Mode

Have you ever found yourself with shaky video footage? Action mode is here to rescue your videos by mimicking image stabilization.

✓ Activating Action Mode

Getting ready for action is a breeze. Launch the native camera app, switch to video mode, and tap the running person icon – voila! You've activated the iPhone Action mode. By default, Action mode uses the ultrawide lens. Still, you can switch to 1080p HD or even 2.8K resolution with a few adjustments.

✓ Challenges in Low Light

Action mode may struggle in low-light conditions, especially indoors. If you're filming in dim surroundings, you might see a 'More Light Required Message' on your screen; this doesn't mean Action mode won't work indoors; it just means the image quality might not be crystal clear.

However, you can improve this by going to Settings, selecting Camera > Record Video, and enabling the 'Action Mode Lower Light' option. This feature will enhance the video quality somewhat, though it may still have some graininess – don't expect Hollywood-level results.

216

✓ Tips for Indoor Action

If you need to use Action mode indoors, try to find a well-lit area for better results. Alternatively, consider whether it's necessary to activate it indoors at all.

## The New Night Mode

Night mode empowers you to capture intricate details in low-light situations. It illuminates your photos and reveals objects that would typically remain concealed in darkness.

✓ Activating Night Mode

Utilizing Night mode is effortless. Launch the camera app, select the Photo mode, and behold, your iPhone automatically activates Night Mode when it senses low-light conditions. Keep an eye on the Night Mode icon at the top of your screen; it will turn a radiant yellow when Night Mode is in operation.

Also, a countdown timer next to the icon informs you of the time required for a Night mode photo. Feel free to toggle Night mode on and off by tapping this icon. However, remember that switching to the Live Photo mode or activating the flash will turn off Night mode.

✓ Customize Your Capture Duration

Night mode offers flexibility in customizing your capture time, allowing you to shape the outcome of your photos. In the example above, the capture time has been extended from three seconds to a more substantial ten seconds.

Here's how you can do it:

Click the arrow located above the viewfinder to access camera settings.

Beneath the viewfinder, you'll find the Night mode button; tap it.

Utilize the slider positioned above the shutter button to select "Max," which maximizes the capture time.

As you snap your photo, the slider transforms into a countdown timer, marking the conclusion of the capture time.

## Portrait Mode and Depth Control

Portrait Mode and Depth Control allow you to capture stunning photos with a blurred background (bokeh) effect.

✓ Taking Portrait Photos with Depth Effect

Open Camera App: Launch the **"Camera"** app on your iPhone.

Select Portrait Mode: Swipe to the **"Portrait"** mode. It's usually found alongside modes like **"Photo"** and **"Video."**

Frame Your Subject: Compose your shot with the subject in the foreground.

Focus: Tap the subject on the screen to ensure the camera focuses on it. You'll see a yellow box around the subject.

Take the Photo: Press the shutter button to capture the photo. The camera will create a portrait photo with a blurred background.

✓ Adjusting Depth Control After Taking Photos

Open Photos App: Launch the **"Photos"** app on your iPhone.

Select a Portrait Photo: Choose the portrait photo you want to adjust.

Edit: Tap "Edit" at the top right corner of the screen.

Depth Control: Below the photo is a **"Depth"** slider. Slide it left or right to adjust the background blur (depth of field).

Save: Tap "Done" to save the adjusted depth control settings.

✓ Editing Portrait Lighting Effects

Open Photos App: Launch the **"Photos"** app on your iPhone.

Select a Portrait Photo: Choose the portrait photo with the Portrait Lighting effects you want to edit.

Edit: Tap **"Edit"** at the top right corner of the screen.

Portrait Lighting: Below the photo, you'll find various Portrait Lighting effects like "Natural Light," "Studio Light," etc. Tap each result to see how it changes the lighting on the subject.

Save: Tap "Done" to save the edited Portrait Lighting effect.

✓ Portrait Mode with Front-Facing Camera

Open Camera App: Launch the **"Camera"** app on your iPhone.

Switch to Selfie Mode: Swipe to the **"Portrait"** mode, then tap the circular arrow icon at the top of the screen to switch to the front-facing camera.

Frame Your Selfie: Compose your selfie with the subject in the foreground.

Focus: Tap the subject on the screen to ensure the camera focuses on it.

Take the Selfie: Press the shutter button to capture the selfie with a blurred background.

## Advanced Camera Tips

Advanced camera tips can help you maximize your iPhone 15 Pro Max camera capabilities.

✓ Using the QR Code Scanner

Access the Camera App: Open your iPhone's **"Camera"** app.

Activate QR Scanner: The QR code scanner is typically activated by default when you open the Camera app. Point your camera at a QR code to scan it. Your iPhone will recognize the code and provide relevant actions, such as opening a website or adding a contact.

✓ Scanning Documents and Saving as PDFs

Open the Notes App: Launch the **"Notes"** app on your iPhone.

Create or Open a Note: Create a new note or open an existing one.

Access the Scanning Tool: Tap the plus icon (**+**) above the keyboard, then select **"Scan Documents."**

Scan the Document: Position your iPhone over the document. The camera will automatically detect the edges and capture the scan. You can adjust the corners if needed.

Save as PDF: After scanning all pages, tap "Save" to save the document as a PDF in your note.

✓ Configure Camera Settings (e.g., Format, Grid)

Open the Settings App: Launch your iPhone's "Settings" app.

Scroll Down and Select Camera: Scroll down and tap "Camera."

Camera Settings: In the Camera settings, you can configure various options such as:

Format: Choose between High Efficiency (HEIF/HEVC) and Most Compatible (JPEG/H.264) image and video formats.

Grid: Enable the grid to help with composition.

Preserve Settings: Customize settings like exposure, filters, and Live Photos.

✓ Creating and Managing Shortcuts for Camera Tasks

Open the Shortcuts App: Launch the "Shortcuts" app by pressing and holding the new Action button.

Create a New Shortcut: Tap the **"+" icon** to create a new shortcut.

Add Actions: Tap "Add Action" to select actions related to the camera. For example, you can add actions to open the camera, take a photo, adjust camera settings, or perform other camera-related tasks.

Configure Actions: Customize the actions to suit your needs. For example, you can set specific camera settings or create shortcuts for certain photography tasks.

Save Shortcut: Once your shortcut is configured, tap **"Next"** and give it a name. Then, tap "Done" to save it.

Use and Manage Shortcuts: You can now use your camera-related shortcuts from the Shortcuts app or add them to your home screen or widgets for quick access.

## Photo and Video Privacy

Protecting your photo and video privacy helps you safeguard personal data and control your media.

Managing Location Data for Photos

Open Settings: Launch the **"Settings"** app on your iPhone.

Privacy Settings: Scroll down and tap **"Privacy."**

Location Services: Tap **"Location Services"** to manage app-specific location permissions.

Camera and Photos: Scroll through the list of apps and adjust the location access for the Camera and Photos app based on your preferences.

✓ Controlling Access to the Camera and Photos:

Open Settings: Launch the **"Settings"** app on your iPhone.

Privacy Settings: Scroll down and tap **"Privacy."**

Camera and Photos: Here, you can control which apps can access your camera and photos. Tap on each app to adjust its permissions. You can choose to allow or deny access.

✓ Privacy Considerations When Sharing Photos

Be Mindful of Metadata: When sharing photos, be aware that they may contain metadata, including location information. Consider using apps or services that strip this metadata before sharing to protect your location privacy.

Private Sharing: Use private sharing methods, such as direct messaging or secure cloud services, when sharing sensitive photos to control who can access them.

✓ Safeguarding Your Media from Unauthorized Access

Enable Passcode or Face ID: Set up a strong passcode or Face ID for your iPhone under **"Settings > Face ID & Passcode;"** this adds an extra layer of security.

Use a Strong Password: If you use a passcode, make sure it's complex and not easily guessable.

Enable Two-Factor Authentication (2FA): Enable 2FA for your Apple ID to protect your iCloud account, where your photos may be stored.

Use Secure Backup Services: If you back up your photos to the cloud, use reputable and secure services like iCloud, Google Photos, or other trusted providers.

Keep Software Updated: Regularly update your iPhone's software to ensure you have the latest security patches.

# CHAPTER TEN

# Using Safari Web Browser

Open Safari: Tap the Safari icon on your iPhone's home screen, which looks like a blue compass.

Navigate to a Website: Tap the URL bar at the top of the screen, enter the website address (e.g., "www.apple.com"), and tap **"Go"** on the keyboard. Safari will load the website.

Navigation: Use familiar gestures like swiping up and down to scroll through webpages and pinch to zoom in or out on a webpage.

✓ Opening and Managing Multiple Tabs

Open a New Tab: Tap the square icon with a **"+"** sign at the bottom right corner of the screen to open a new tab. You can also tap and hold the tabs icon (two overlapping squares) at the bottom to reveal options for opening new tabs.

Switch Between Tabs: Swipe left or right on the open tabs at the top of the screen to switch between them.

Close Tabs: To close a tab, tap the **"X"** icon on the top left corner of the tab. To close all tabs simultaneously, tap and hold the tabs icon, then select **"Close All X Tabs."**

✓ Using Bookmarks and Favorites

Add a Bookmark: While on a webpage, tap the share icon (square with an upward-pointing arrow) at the bottom of the screen, then select **"Add Bookmark."** You can choose the bookmark location and edit its name.

Access Bookmarks: Tap the bookmarks icon (an open book) at the bottom of the screen to access your bookmarks. You can organize them into folders and access your favorite websites quickly.

✓ Accessing the Reading List and History

Reading List: To add a webpage to your Reading List, tap the share icon and select **"Add to Reading List."** To access it later, tap the bookmarks icon, then go to the **"Reading List"** tab.

History: To view your browsing history, tap the bookmarks icon, then go to the **"History"** tab. You can see a list of recently visited websites and tap on them to revisit.

# Browsing Tips and Tricks

Becoming skilled at browsing tips and tricks in Safari can enhance your web experience.

✓ Zooming and Adjusting Text Size

Zoom In/Out: To zoom in on a webpage, double tap with two fingers on the screen. To zoom out, double-tap again. You can also use the familiar pinch-to-zoom gesture by placing two fingers on the screen and spreading them apart to zoom in or pinching them together to zoom out.

Adjust Text Size: You can change the text size of a webpage by going to **"Settings > Display & Brightness > Text Size"** and adjusting the slider to your preferred size. Safari will remember this setting for future browsing.

✓ Using Private Browsing Mode

Open Safari: Launch Safari on your iPhone.

Activate Private Browsing: Tap the tabs icon at the bottom right corner (it looks like two overlapping squares). Then, tap **"Private"** at the bottom left corner; this will open a new private browsing tab.

Browsing Privately: While in private browsing mode, Safari won't save your browsing history, cookies, or other data. You can tell you're in private mode by the dark theme and the "Private" label on the address bar.

✓ Requesting Desktop Websites

Open Safari: Launch Safari on your iPhone.

Access a Website: Navigate to the website you want to view in desktop mode.

Request Desktop Site: Tap and hold the refresh icon in the address bar (it looks like a circular arrow). A menu will appear, allowing you to select **"Request Desktop Site."** Safari will reload the page as if you were on a desktop computer.

✓ Enabling and Managing Content Blockers

Open Settings: Launch the **"Settings"** app on your iPhone.

Scroll Down and Select Safari: Scroll down to find the Safari settings.

Content Blockers: Tap **"Content Blockers"** to view and manage any content-blocking apps or extensions you have installed. You can toggle them on or off.

**Note:** Content blockers can help improve your browsing experience by blocking ads and other unwanted website content.

## Managing Downloads and Files

Managing downloads and files is essential for organizing and accessing your digital content.

✓ Downloading Files, Images, and Documents

Navigate to the Content: Use Safari or any other app that allows file downloads to navigate to the content you want to download (e.g., a PDF, image, or document).

Download: Tap on the link to the file. It will open in a viewer depending on the file type or prompt you to download it. If prompted, tap **"Download."**

✓ Accessing and Managing Downloads

Files App: The Files app on your iPhone allows you to access and manage downloaded files. Open the **"Files" app** from your home screen.

Downloads Location: By default, files are saved in the "Downloads" folder. Tap on "Downloads" to access your downloaded files.

Organize and Manage: You can create folders, move files, rename them, and delete them within the Files app.

✓ Saving Web Pages and Articles for Offline Reading

Access Web Content: Use Safari to navigate to the web page or article you want to save for offline reading.

Share Button: Tap the share button (square with an upward-pointing arrow) at the bottom of the screen.

Save PDF to Files: Scroll down in the share sheet to find the option to **"Save PDF to Files."** Tap it.

Choose Location: Select the location in the Files app where you want to save the PDF, then tap **"Add."**

✓ Sharing Web Content with Other Apps

Access Web Content: Use Safari to navigate the web page or content you want to share with another app.

Share Button: Tap the share button (square with an upward-pointing arrow) at the bottom of the screen.

Select App: In the share sheet, choose the app you want to share the content with (e.g., Messages, Mail, Notes, or a third-party app).

Customize Sharing: Depending on the app you choose, you may be able to customize the sharing by adding a message or selecting specific recipients.

## Managing Passwords and Autofill

Managing passwords and autofill options is vital for security and convenience.

✓ Setting Up and Using Third-Party Password Managers

Install a Password Manager: Download and install a reputable third-party password manager app from the App Store (e.g., 1Password, LastPass, or Dashlane).

Create an Account: Open the app and create an account. Follow the app's setup instructions.

Import or Manually Add Passwords: You can import existing passwords or manually add new ones, depending on the app.

Use Autofill: The password manager will integrate with your iPhone's autofill feature. When you encounter login forms, your password manager will offer to fill in your credentials.

✓ Configuring Autofill Options for Forms and Passwords

Open Settings: Launch the **"Settings"** app on your iPhone.

Passwords & Accounts: Scroll down and tap **"Passwords & Accounts."**

Autofill Passwords: Tap **"Autofill Passwords."**

Select Password Manager: Choose the password manager you want to use for autofill. You can also turn **on/off "Keychain"** here.

Web Forms: To configure autofill for web forms, go to **"Settings > Safari > Autofill."** You can turn on/off the options for Names and Passwords.

✓ Managing Saved Passwords and Accounts

iCloud Keychain: To manage passwords saved in iCloud Keychain, go to **"Settings > Passwords & Accounts > Website & App Passwords."** Here, you can view, edit, or delete saved passwords.

Third-Party Password Managers: For third-party password managers, open the app, and you'll find options to view and manage saved passwords and accounts within the app.

## Search and Navigation

Effective search and navigation help you find information and get around.

✓ Conducting Web Searches in Safari

Open Safari: Launch the **"Safari" app** on your iPhone.

Search Bar: Tap the URL bar at the top of the screen.

Enter Search Query: Type your search query (e.g., "best restaurants in my area") and tap "Go" on the keyboard.

Search Results: Safari will display search results from your chosen search engine (usually Google). Tap on a search result to view the webpage.

✓ Using Voice Search with Siri

Activate Siri: Either say "Hey Siri" (if you have this feature enabled) or press and hold the side button (or home button if you have one) to activate Siri.

Voice Query: Speak your search query, such as "Find Italian restaurants near me."

Results: Siri will provide spoken search results and display them on the screen. You can tap on the results for more details.

✓ Navigating with Maps and Location-Based Services

Open Maps: Launch the "Maps" app on your iPhone.

Enter Destination: Tap the search bar at the top of the screen and enter your destination (e.g., "Times Square").

Route Options: Maps will display route options. Tap on the one you prefer.

Start Navigation: Tap "Start" to begin turn-by-turn navigation. You'll receive voice and visual directions.

✓ Finding Businesses and Directions

Open Maps: Launch the "Maps" app on your iPhone.

Search for Business: In the search bar, enter the name or type of business you're looking for (e.g., "coffee shop").

Observe Results: Maps will display businesses that match your search. Tap on a result to view details.

Get Directions: Once you've selected a business, tap "Directions" to get directions to that location.

Share Directions: You can also tap the share icon to send directions to others via messages or other apps.

## Privacy and Security

Protecting your privacy and security while browsing in Safari is vital because:

Prevent Cross-Site Tracking: Safari automatically prevents websites from tracking your activity across different sites. You can enable this feature by going to **"Settings > Safari > Prevent Cross-Site Tracking."**

Intelligent Tracking Prevention (ITP): Safari uses ITP to block cookies and other tracking mechanisms from being used to build user profiles.

✓ Managing Cookies and Website Data

Open Settings: Launch the **"Settings"** app on your iPhone.

Scroll Down and Select Safari: Scroll down and tap **"Safari."**

Privacy & Security: Under **"Privacy & Security,"** you have several options:

Block All Cookies: You can block all cookies, but this may affect the functionality of some websites.

Prevent Cross-Site Tracking: As mentioned earlier, you can enable this feature to prevent tracking.

Ask Websites Not to Track Me: This option informs websites that you don't want to be tracked.

Manage Website Data: To view and manage specific website data, tap **"Advanced > Website Data."** You can delete data for definite websites or remove all website data.

✓ Blocking Pop-Ups and Fraudulent Websites

Open Settings: Launch the **"Settings"** app on your iPhone.

Scroll Down and Select Safari: Scroll down and tap **"Safari."**

Block Pop-ups: Enable the **"Block Pop-ups"** option to prevent pop-up windows from appearing while browsing.

Fraudulent Website Warning: Enable the "Fraudulent Website Warning" option to be alerted if Safari detects a website that may be trying to trick you into disclosing personal information.

✓ Ensuring Secure Browsing and Data Protection

HTTPS: Ensure that websites you visit use **"https://"** in their URLs. Safari automatically provides a secure connection to such websites.

Use Strong Passwords: Use strong, unique passwords when creating accounts or logging in to websites. Consider using a password manager to generate and store them securely.

Regular Software Updates: Keep your iPhone's software up to date. Apple regularly releases security updates.

Two-Factor Authentication (2FA): Enable 2FA for your Apple ID and other online accounts whenever possible to add an extra layer of security.

## Web App Integration

Integrating web apps into your iPhone 15 Pro Max can enhance your web experience.

✓ Adding Websites to the Home Screen as Web Apps

Open Safari: Launch the **"Safari" app** on your iPhone.

Navigate to the Website: Use Safari to go to the website you want to add to your home screen.

Share Button: Tap the share button (square with an upward-pointing arrow) at the bottom of the screen.

Add to Home Screen: Scroll down in the share sheet to find the option to **"Add to Home Screen."** Tap it.

Name the Web App: You can edit the name of the web app if you like. Once done, tap **"Add."**

Shortcut on Home Screen: A shortcut icon for the web app will be added to your home screen. You can move it and place it like any other app icon.

✓ Using Progressive Web Apps (PWAs)

PWAs are web apps designed to work like native apps on your iPhone.

Access a PWA: Open Safari and navigate to a PWA-enabled website (e.g., Reddit, Airbnb, or Amazon).

Add to Home Screen: Follow the abovementioned steps for adding websites to the home screen as web apps. PWAs often provide this option automatically.

Use Like a Native App: Once added to your home screen, you can launch the PWA like a native app. It may have offline capabilities and a more app-like experience.

✓ Managing Web App Shortcuts and Updates

Home Screen: All web app shortcuts are placed on your home screen, like native app icons. You can organize and manage them as you do with other apps.

Updates: Web apps typically update themselves when you access them. There's no need to update them from the App Store manually. However, you should clear your cache and data occasionally to ensure you're using the latest version of the web app.

✓ Removing Web Apps When No Longer Needed

Hold and Delete: To remove a web app shortcut from your home screen, tap and hold the icon until it starts wiggling. Then, confirm the deletion by tapping the **"X"** in the icon's corner.

Uninstall PWAs: Delete the shortcut described above if you've added a PWA and no longer need it.

## Notifications and Alerts

Open Safari: Launch the **"Safari"** app on your iPhone.

Visit a Website: Navigate to the website for which you want to configure notifications.

Allow Notifications: When you visit a website that offers notifications, Safari may ask if you want to allow notifications. You'll typically see a pop-up at the top of the screen. Tap **"Allow"** to enable notifications for that site.

✓ Managing Website Permissions

Open Settings: Launch the **"Settings"** app on your iPhone.

Scroll Down and Select Safari: Scroll down and tap **"Safari."**

Website Settings: Under **"Settings for Websites,"** you'll find various options for managing website permissions, including:

Location: Control which websites can access your area.

Camera and Microphone: Manage access to your device's camera and microphone by websites.

Motion and Orientation Access: Control which sites can access your device's motion and orientation data.

Downloads: Determine if websites can ask to download files.

✓ Handling Alerts and Notifications While Browsing

Receive Notifications: When you've allowed notifications for a website, you'll receive alerts or banners when new content or updates are available. You can tap these notifications to open the website directly.

Manage Notifications: Go to **"Settings > Safari > Notifications** to manage website notifications." Here, you can view a list of websites with notification permissions and toggle them on or off.

Clear Notifications: Swipe down from the top of the screen to access your Notification Center. You can clear notifications individually or all at once.

✓ Controlling Push Notifications

Open Settings: Launch the **"Settings"** app on your iPhone.

Scroll Down and Select Notifications: Scroll down and tap **"Notifications."**

App Notifications: Scroll through the list of apps and find the one related to the website or service you want to 'control' push notifications for.

Configure Notifications: Tap the app, and you can configure its notification settings, including notification style, sounds, badges, and whether or not to show notifications on the lock screen.

Turn Off Notifications: To turn off push notifications entirely for a specific app, toggle off the "Allow Notifications" switch.

# CHAPTER ELEVEN

# Using iMessage and SMS

Open Messages: Launch the **"Messages"** app on your iPhone.

Start a New Message: Tap the compose icon (pencil icon) in the upper right corner of the screen.

Recipient: Enter the recipient's name or phone number in the "To:" field. You can also tap the **"+"** **icon** to select recipients from your contacts.

Type Your Message: Tap the text field at the bottom of the screen and type your message.

Send: Tap the blue send button (a blue upward-pointing arrow) to send your iMessage.

✓ Sending SMS (Text Messages)

Open Messages: Launch the **"Messages"** app on your iPhone.

Start a New Message: Follow the same steps as for composing iMessages.

Recipient: If the recipient has iMessage, your message will be sent as an iMessage. If not, it will automatically switch to SMS if you have cellular connectivity.

Type Your Message: Enter your text in the same way as you would for iMessages.

Send: Tap the send button (the blue upward-pointing arrow) to send your SMS.

✓ Receiving and Reading Messages

Message Notification: When someone sends you a message, you'll receive a notification on your lock screen, in the Notification Center, and as a badge on the Messages app icon.

Read Messages: Tap the notification or open the Messages app to read the message. Messages you haven't read yet will be marked with a blue dot.

✓ Managing Message Conversations and Threads

Open Messages: Launch the "Messages" app.

View Conversations: You'll see a list of your message conversations. Tap a conversation to view its thread.

Delete Messages: To delete a single message, tap and hold the message, then select **"More"** and choose **"Delete."** To delete an entire conversation, swipe left on it in the conversation list and tap "Delete."

Archive Messages: You can archive conversations by swiping left and tapping "Archive;" this moves them to the archived folder.

Search Messages: You can search for specific messages or conversations by tapping the search icon (a magnifying glass) at the top of the conversation list.

## Setting Up and Managing Email Accounts

You can stay connected by setting up and managing your iPhone 15 Pro Max email accounts.

✓ Adding an Email Account to the Mail App

Open Settings: Launch the **"Settings"** app on your iPhone.

Scroll Down and Select Mail: Scroll down the list of settings and tap **"Mail."**

Accounts: Under the **"Accounts"** section, tap **"Add Account."**

Select Email Provider: Choose your email provider (e.g., Google, iCloud, Yahoo, Microsoft Exchange, or Other).

Sign In: Enter your email address and password for the chosen account.

Configure Account: Follow the on-screen instructions to configure your account settings, including name, email address, server information, and more.

Save: Tap **"Next"** or **"Sign In"** to save your settings and add the account.

✓ Configuring POP or IMAP Settings

POP or IMAP: When adding an email account, you may need to select between POP (Post Office Protocol) or IMAP (Internet Message Access Protocol) settings. IMAP is typically preferred as it syncs your emails across devices.

Server Settings: You must provide server settings for incoming (IMAP/POP) and outgoing (SMTP) emails. Consult your email provider for these settings.

✓ Setting Up Gmail, iCloud, and Other Popular Email Providers

Gmail: For Gmail, choose the **"Google"** option when adding an account. Enter your Gmail email and password, and the setup process will guide you.

iCloud: To set up an iCloud email account, choose **"iCloud"** and sign in with your Apple ID. iCloud email is automatically configured.

✓ Syncing Multiple Email Accounts

Repeat the Process: To add multiple email accounts, repeat the above process for each additional account.

Mailboxes: In the Mail app, you can access all your email accounts by tapping the "Mailboxes" button at the top left and selecting the account you want to use.

## Composing and Sending Emails

Composing and sending emails is a fundamental aspect of staying connected.

Open Mail App: Launch the "Mail" app on your iPhone.

Compose Email: Tap the compose icon (pencil icon) in the screen's bottom right corner.

Recipient(s): In the "To:" field, enter the recipient's email address. You can add multiple recipients by separating their email addresses with commas.

Subject: Tap the subject field to enter a subject for your email; this is typically a summary of the email's content.

Compose Message: In the main message field, type your email message. You can format text, add links, and use various formatting options like bold, italic, and underline.

✓ Attaching Files, Photos, and Documents

Compose Email: Create a new email or reply to an existing one.

Tap and Hold: In the email composition screen, tap and hold in the body of the email where you want to insert an attachment.

Insert Photo or Video: Choose "Insert Photo or Video" to attach an image or video from your device's gallery.

Insert Document: To attach a document from iCloud Drive or other cloud storage services, tap "Insert Document."

Browse and Select: Browse your device or cloud storage to select the file you want to attach, then tap "Choose."

✓ Sending Emails with or Without Recipients' Names

Recipient(s): In the "To:" field, you can enter the recipient's email address. However, you can also send emails without specifying a name using a general email address.

Generic Addresses: If you want to email a department or group, you can use a generic address like "support@company.com" or "sales@organization.org."

✓ Using the Cc and Bcc Fields

Cc (Carbon Copy): To add recipients who should receive a copy of the email for information purposes, tap "Cc/Bcc" below the "To:" field. Enter email addresses in the "Cc" field.

Bcc (Blind Carbon Copy): Bcc is used to send copies of the email without other recipients knowing. Tap "Cc/Bcc" to add Bcc recipients and enter email addresses in the "Bcc" field.

Additional Recipients: You can add multiple addresses to the "Cc" and "Bcc" fields.

Finish Composing: Complete your email, and when you're ready, tap "Send."

# Organizing and Managing Email

Open Mail App: Launch the "Mail" app on your iPhone.

Inbox: Your inbox displays all your incoming emails.

Organize Emails: To organize emails, tap "Edit" in the top right corner of the inbox. You can select multiple emails by tapping the circle icon next to each email.

Actions: Once you've selected emails, you can take various actions using the options at the bottom of the screen. These actions include moving, deleting, archiving, or marking emails.

✓ Creating and Using Folders or Labels

Create a Folder (Mailboxes): In the Mail app, tap **"Mailboxes"** in the top left corner of the screen.

Edit: Tap "Edit" in the top right corner.

New Mailbox: Tap "New Mailbox" to create a new folder.

Name Folder: Name the folder and choose where to create it (On My iPhone or an email account).

Save: Tap "Save" to create the folder.

Move Emails: To move emails to a folder, open the email, tap the folder icon at the bottom, and select the destination folder.

✓ Marking Emails as Read or Unread

Inbox: Open your inbox in the Mail app.

Select Email: Tap and hold the email you want to mark.

Mark as Read/Unread: From the menu that appears, choose "Mark as Read" or "Mark as Unread."

✓ Archiving and Deleting Emails

Open Email: Open the email you want to archive or delete.

Archive: To archive an email, tap the folder icon at the bottom and select "Archive;" this moves the email to the All Mail folder (in Gmail) or the Archive folder (in some other email services).

Delete: To delete an email, tap the trash can icon at the bottom. Deleted emails are usually moved to the Trash or Deleted Items folder.

Empty Trash: To permanently delete emails from the Trash folder, go to the Trash folder, tap "Edit," and then tap "Delete All."

## Searching for Emails

Open Mail App: Launch the "Mail" app on your iPhone 15 Pro Max.

Inbox or Folder: Go to the inbox or folder where you want to search for emails.

Search Bar: There's a search bar at the top of the screen. Tap on it.

Enter Search Terms: Enter keywords, sender's name, or other relevant search terms.

Search: Tap "Search" on the keyboard. Your search results will appear below the search bar.

✓ Using Filters and Sorting Options

Search Filters: After entering your search terms, tap "Filters" to refine your search. You can filter by sender, subject, mailbox, and more.

Sorting Options: You can also sort your search results by date, sender, subject, or relevance by tapping "Sort by."

✓ Searching Within Attachments

Open Search: Start a search as described above.

Attachments: To search within attachments, enter keywords related to the content within the attachment in the search bar.

Review Results: The search results will include emails with attachments that match your search criteria.

✓ Saving Search Results for Future Reference

Search: Follow the steps above to perform your search.

Bookmarks: Once you've obtained search results, you can save them for future reference. Tap "Edit" in the top right corner and then "Save" to add the search to your bookmarks.

Access Saved Searches: To access saved searches, go to the "Mailboxes" screen, scroll down to "Search," and find your saved searches there.

## Email Notifications and Alerts

Configuring email notifications and alerts helps you stay on top of your emails without being overwhelmed.

✓ Email Notification Settings

Open Settings: Launch the "Settings" app on your iPhone.

Scroll Down and Select Mail: Scroll down and tap "Mail."

Notifications: Under "Notifications," tap the email account for which you want to configure notifications.

Allow Notifications: Toggle "Allow Notifications" to enable notifications for this email account.

Notification Sound: You can select the notification sound by tapping "Sound" and choosing from the available options.

Badge App Icon: Toggle the "Badge App Icon" to display the number of unread emails on the Mail app icon.

Show in Notification Center: You can choose to show email notifications in the Notification Center by toggling on "Show in Notification Center."

✓ Managing Alerts and Sounds

Open Settings: Launch the "Settings" app.

Sounds & Haptics: Scroll Down and Select "Sounds & Haptics."

Email Alerts: You can customize the sound for email alerts by scrolling down to the "New Mail" section and selecting a sound.

✓ Handling Email Notifications on the Lock Screen

Lock Screen Notifications: When you receive an email notification, it will appear on your lock screen. You can tap the information to open the email directly.

Preview: If you want to control the level of detail shown in email notifications on the lock screen, go to **"Settings > Mail > Notifications"** and select the email account. You can choose to show previews or hide them.

✓ Snooze and Priority Features

Snooze Emails: In the Mail app, swipe an email to the left and tap "More" to access the "Snooze" feature; this allows you to temporarily remove an email from your inbox and set a time for it to reappear.

Priority Inbox: You can set up a priority inbox by going to "Settings > Mail > Priority Inbox." Here, you can configure rules to identify requisite emails and move them to a separate folder for easier access.

## Managing Email Attachments

Managing email attachments helps you handle files and documents efficiently.

✓ Opening and Saving Attachments

Open Mail App: Launch the "Mail" app on your iPhone.

Open Email: Tap the email containing the attachment you want to open.

Tap Attachment: To open an attachment, tap it. It will open in the appropriate app for that file type.

Save Attachment: To save an attachment, tap and hold it, then select "Save Attachment." You can save it to your iCloud Drive, On My iPhone, or another location.

✓ Sending Attachments from Email

Compose Email: Open the Mail app and tap the compose icon (pencil icon) to create a new email.

Attach File: Tap and hold in the email body where you want to attach the file. Select "Add Attachment" and choose the file you want to link.

Finish Email: Complete the email and tap "Send" to send it with the attachment.

✓ Sharing Attachments with Other Apps

Open Email: Go to the email with the attachment you want to share.

Tap Attachment: Tap the attachment to open it.

Share: Look for a share icon in the app where the attachment is displayed (usually a square with an arrow pointing up). Tap it to share the attachment with other apps, like Messages, Notes, or a cloud storage service like Dropbox or Google Drive.

✓ Managing Storage Space for Attachments

Open Settings: Launch the "Settings" app on your iPhone.

Scroll Down and Select Mail: Scroll down and tap "Mail."

Attachments: Under "Messages," you can manage how long attachments are kept in your email. Choose "Keep Messages" and select a duration (30 Days, 1 Year, or Forever).

Clear Old Attachments: To manually clear old attachments, go to the email conversation, tap and hold an attachment, and select "Remove" to delete it; this can free up storage space.

## Email Security and Privacy

Ensuring the security and privacy of your email account is of high importance.

✓ Recognizing Phishing and Scam Emails

Check the Sender: Be cautious of emails from unknown senders or suspicious-looking email addresses.

Look for Spelling and Grammar Mistakes: Phishing emails often contain errors in spelling and grammar.

Avoid Clicking Suspicious Links: Don't click links or download attachments in emails you weren't expecting.

Verify Requests for Personal Information: Legitimate organizations will not ask you to provide sensitive information (e.g., passwords, social security numbers) via email.

Check the URL: Hover your mouse over links (without clicking) to see the actual web address. Ensure it matches the official website of the sender.

Protecting Your Email Account with a Strong Password:

Change Password: Go to your email account settings and change your password regularly.

Use Strong Passwords: Create strong passwords that combine letters, numbers, and special characters.

Avoid Common Passwords: Avoid easily guessable passwords like "password123" or "123456."

Use a Password Manager: Consider using a password manager app to securely generate and store strong passwords.

✓ Enabling Two-Factor Authentication (2FA)

Open Settings: Launch the "Settings" app on your iPhone.

Scroll Down and Select Passwords & Accounts: Tap "Passwords & Accounts."

Account: Tap the email account you want to secure with 2FA.

Turn on Two-Factor Authentication: Look for the option to enable two-factor authentication and follow the setup process; this usually involves receiving a code via SMS or using an authenticator app.

✓ Managing Email Account Permissions

Open Settings: Launch the "Settings" app on your iPhone.

Scroll Down and Select Mail: Scroll down and tap "Mail."

Accounts: Under "Accounts," tap the email account you want to manage permissions for.

Account Permissions: Here, you can review and manage the permissions granted to the email account, including access to contacts, calendars, and other features. Adjust these settings as needed for privacy.

## Multiple Email Accounts and Unified Inbox

Managing multiple email accounts and having a unified inbox can streamline your email

✓ Handling Multiple Email Accounts

Open Mail App: Launch the "Mail" app on your iPhone 15 Pro Max.

Mailboxes: In the Mail app, tap "Mailboxes" at the top left corner. You'll see a list of your email accounts and folders.

Switch Accounts: Tap the desired account in the list to switch between email accounts; this allows you to access each account's inbox, sent items, and other folders.

✓ Setting Up a Unified Inbox (Optional)

Open Mail App: Launch the "Mail" app on your iPhone.

Mailboxes: In the Mail app, tap "Mailboxes" at the top left corner.

Unified Inbox: Scroll down in the Mailboxes list and tap "All Inboxes;" this will create a unified inbox that combines emails from all your accounts.

View Unified Inbox: To switch to the unified inbox, tap "All Inboxes" in the Mailboxes list. You can easily change back to individual accounts when needed.

✓ Managing Sent Items Across Accounts

Open Mail App: Launch the "Mail" app on your iPhone.

Sent Items: When you send an email from any of your accounts, a copy is automatically saved in the "Sent" folder for that specific account.

View Sent Items: To view sent items for a specific account, go to the account's folder list and tap "Sent."

✓ Syncing Calendars and Contacts

Open Settings: Launch the "Settings" app on your iPhone.

Passwords & Accounts: Scroll down and tap "Passwords & Accounts."

Accounts: Tap the email account for which you want to sync calendars and contacts.

Toggle on Contacts and Calendars: Make sure "Contacts" and "Calendars" are toggled on to sync these data types with your iPhone.

Sync Frequency: You can adjust the sync frequency and choose how far back in time to sync events and contacts.

# CHAPTER TWELVE

# Making and Receiving Calls

Making and receiving calls are fundamental functions of your iPhone 15 Pro Max.

✓ Dialing a Phone Number

Unlock Your Phone: Wake up your iPhone by pressing the sleep/wake button or using Face ID.

Open the Phone App: Locate and tap the green "Phone" icon on your home screen or in your app drawer.

Dial a Number: In the Phone app, tap the keypad icon at the bottom. Use the on-screen keypad to dial the number you want to call.

Call: Tap the green "Call" button to initiate the call.

✓ Receiving Incoming Calls

Incoming Call: When you receive an incoming call, your iPhone will display the caller's name or number on the screen.

Accept Call: To answer the call, tap the green "Accept" button on the screen or press the side button (on the right side of the phone) or the volume up button.

Decline Call: To decline the call, tap the red "Decline" button on the screen or press the side or volume down button.

Silence Call: To silence an incoming call, press the volume or sleep/wake buttons.

✓ Managing Call Options

During a call, you can access several options

Speakerphone: Tap the "Speaker" icon to use the speakerphone.

Mute: Tap the "Mute" button to mute your microphone.

Add Call: To add another call to the current call, tap "Add Call" and dial the second number.

Hold: Tap "Hold" to place the current call on hold.

✓ Ending a Call and Call History

End Call: To end a call, tap the red "End" button on the screen or press the side button.

Call History: To access your call history, open the Phone app and tap the "Recents" tab at the bottom. Here, you can see a list of your recent calls, including missed, received, and dialed calls.

## Sending and Receiving Text Messages

Open Messages App: Locate and tap the green "Messages" icon on your home screen or in your app drawer.

Compose a Message: Tap the compose icon (pencil icon), usually in the top right or bottom right corner of the Messages app.

Enter Recipient: In the "To:" field, enter the recipient's phone number or tap the "+" icon to select a contact.

Compose Message: Tap in the main message field and type your message.

Send: Tap the blue arrow or "Send" button to send the message.

✓ Receiving and Reading Text Messages

Incoming Message: When you receive an SMS, it will appear in the Messages app.

Read Message: Tap the conversation to open and read the message.

Managing Conversations and Threads

Open Messages App: Launch the "Messages" app on your iPhone.

View Conversations: The main screen displays a list of your message conversations.

Open Conversation: Tap a conversation to view the messages and send replies.

Delete Conversation: To delete a conversation, swipe left on the conversation and tap "Delete."

✓ Using Multimedia Messages (MMS)

Compose a Message: Follow the steps to compose a message (as described above).

Attach Media: Tap the camera icon next to the message input field to send a multimedia message. You can then take a photo or video or choose an existing one from your gallery.

Send Media: After selecting or capturing the media, tap the blue arrow or "Send" button to send the MMS.

## Managing Contacts and Favorites

Open Contacts App: Launch the "Contacts" app on your iPhone.

Add Contact: Tap the "+" icon in the top right or bottom right corner.

Enter Details: Fill in the contact's details, including name, phone number, email, address, etc.

Save: Tap "Done" or "Save" to save the contact.

✓ Importing Contacts from Other Sources

Open Settings: Launch the "Settings" app on your iPhone.

Scroll Down and Select Contacts: Scroll down and tap "Contacts."

Import Contacts: Under "Contacts," you can configure accounts like iCloud, Google, or other email accounts to sync contacts; this will import contacts from those accounts onto your iPhone.

✓ Editing Contact Details

Open Contacts App: Launch the "Contacts" app on your iPhone.

Select Contact: Tap the contact you want to edit.

Edit Details: Tap "Edit" in the top right corner. You can now edit the contact's details.

Save Changes: After making edits, tap "Done" or "Save" to save the changes.

✓ Creating and Managing Favorites or Speed Dial

Open Phone App: Launch the "Phone" app on your iPhone.

Favorites: Tap the "Favorites" tab at the bottom.

Add Favorites: To add a contact to favorites, tap the "+" icon and select a contact from your list.

Reorder Favorites: You can tap "Edit" to rearrange the order of your favorites.

Speed Dial: To use speed dial, assign a contact to a specific number (e.g., 1 to 9) in your favorites. Then, you can tap and hold a number on the keypad in the Phone app to quickly call that contact.

## Setting Up and Using Voicemail

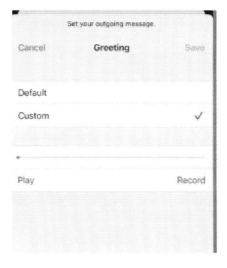

Open Phone App: Launch the "Phone" app on your iPhone.

Voicemail Tab: Tap the "Voicemail" tab at the bottom.

Set Up Greeting: If it's your first time setting up voicemail, you'll be prompted to create a greeting. Follow the on-screen instructions to record and set up your voicemail greeting.

✓ Retrieving and Listening to Voicemail Messages

Open Phone App: Launch the "Phone" app on your iPhone.

Voicemail Tab: Tap the "Voicemail" tab at the bottom.

Listen to Voicemail: You'll see a list of voicemail messages. Tap a voicemail to listen to it.

✓ Managing Voicemail Settings

Open Phone App: Launch the "Phone" app on your iPhone.

Voicemail Tab: Tap the "Voicemail" tab at the bottom.

Voicemail Settings: In the Voicemail tab, tap "Greeting" to change or re-record your greeting or "Voicemail" to access settings like passwords, notifications, and more.

✓ Visual Voicemail

Open Phone App: Launch the "Phone" app on your iPhone.

Voicemail Tab: Tap the "Voicemail" tab at the bottom.

Visual Voicemail: Visual voicemail allows you to see a list of your voicemail messages and choose which ones to listen to or delete.

Play Messages: Tap a voicemail to play it. You can pause, rewind, and delete voicemails as needed.

## Messaging Apps and Third-Party Services

App Store: Open the "App Store" on your iPhone 15 Pro Max.

Search: Use the search bar to find messaging apps like WhatsApp, Facebook Messenger, or any other messaging app you want to explore.

Download: Tap the app you want to try and tap "Get" to download and install it.

✓ Using Third-Party Messaging Services

Open Messaging App: After downloading a messaging app, open it from your home screen.

Sign In/Register: Follow the on-screen instructions to sign in or register for an account within the app.

Setup and Customize: Configure your profile, notification settings, and privacy preferences as needed.

Start Messaging: Find contacts or friends within the app and start messaging.

✓ Syncing Contacts with Messaging Apps

Permissions: When you open a messaging app, it may request access to your contacts. Grant permission to sync your phone's contacts with the app.

Manually Add Contacts: If some contacts don't sync automatically, you can manually add them within the messaging app.

✓ Privacy and Security Considerations

Privacy Settings: Review the privacy settings within the messaging app. You can often customize who can see your information and how your data is used.

Encryption: Many messaging apps offer end-to-end encryption for your messages, ensuring they can only be read by you and the recipient.

Two-Factor Authentication (2FA): Enable 2FA if the messaging app supports it for an extra layer of security.

Message Safety: Be cautious about sharing sensitive information over messaging apps, even encrypted ones. Use secure channels for delicate discussions.

Regular Updates: Keep your messaging apps updated to benefit from security patches and new features.

## Focus Mode and Call Blocking

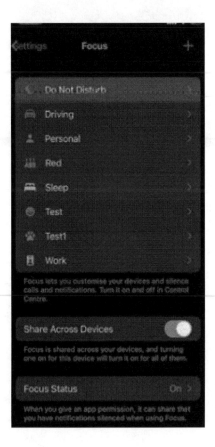

Focus Mode and call-blocking features on your iPhone 15 Pro Max help you manage notifications and block unwanted calls and messages.

✓ Enabling Focus Mode

Open Settings: Launch the "Settings" app on your iPhone.

Focus: Scroll down and tap "Focus" in the list of settings.

Select Focus Mode: Choose the Focus mode that suits your current activity, such as "Personal," "Work," or a custom mode.

Customize Mode: If you select a custom mode, you can further customize the settings based on your preferences.

Turn On Focus: Tap the toggle switch to turn on Focus mode.

✓ Customizing Focus Settings

Open Settings: Launch the "Settings" app on your iPhone.

Focus: Scroll down and tap "Focus."

Select Focus Mode: Choose the Focus mode you want to customize.

Customize Settings: You can customize notifications, calls, and apps for this Focus mode. Adjust the settings to suit your needs.

✓ Blocking Unwanted Calls and Messages

Open Settings: Launch the "Settings" app on your iPhone.

Phone: Scroll down and tap "Phone."

Call Blocking & Identification: Tap "Call Blocking & Identification."

Block Contact: To block a contact, tap "Block Contact" and select the contact you want to stop from your contacts list.

✓ Managing Blocked Contacts

Open Settings: Launch the "Settings" app on your iPhone.

Phone: Scroll down and tap "Phone."

Call Blocking & Identification: Tap "Call Blocking & Identification."

Blocked Contacts: You will see a list of contacts you've stopped. You can unblock contacts by swiping left on their name and tapping "Unblock."

## Setting Up eSIM

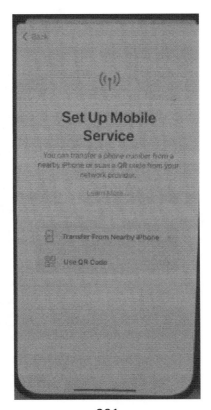

Open Settings: Unlock your iPhone 15 Pro Max and open the "Settings" app from your home screen.

Cellular: Scroll down in the settings menu and tap "Cellular."

Cellular Plans: Under the Cellular section, tap "Cellular Plans."

Add Cellular Plan: On the Cellular Plans screen, tap "Add Cellular Plan." If you don't see this option, your carrier doesn't support eSIM, or your device may not be eligible for eSIM activation.

✓ Scan QR Code or Enter Details Manually

Scan QR Code: If your carrier provided a QR code for eSIM activation, scan it using your iPhone's camera. The phone will automatically recognize and set up the eSIM profile.

Enter Details Manually: If your carrier provided you with details to enter manually, select "Enter Details Manually" and input the information as required; this typically includes the activation code and other details provided by your carrier.

Confirm and Activate: After scanning the QR code or entering the details, your iPhone will prompt you to confirm the activation. Review the information, and if it's correct, tap "Confirm" or "Activate."

Label the eSIM: You can label the eSIM to distinguish it from your physical SIM card if you have one. Choose a label or customize it if needed.

Complete Setup: Once the eSIM activation is full, your iPhone will display a message confirming that the eSIM has been added successfully.

Your eSIM is now set up and active. You can make calls, send messages, and use data as you usually would with a physical SIM card.

# Emergency SOS Via Satellite

Apple introduced a feature on the iPhone 14 Pro Max last year that allows you to reach out to emergency services through satellites, ensuring you can seek help even in scenarios where your cellular network is unavailable. If you have an unobstructed view of the sky, activating Emergency SOS via Satellite is your lifeline in critical situations.

Here's a step-by-step guide on how to explore the functionality of Emergency SOS via Satellite on your iPhone 15 Pro Max:

- ✓ Begin by launching the Settings app on your iPhone 15 Pro Max.
- ✓ Scroll down the menu and locate the Emergency SOS option.
- ✓ Keep scrolling until you reach the section dedicated to Emergency SOS via Satellite.
- ✓ Tap the "Try Demo" button to initiate the demonstration.
- ✓ Follow the tutorial, which previews how this feature operates in real emergencies.
- ✓ Tap the "Test Satellite Connection" button when prompted.
- ✓ Respond by tapping the "Turn off" button to temporarily undo cellular connectivity for testing purposes.
- ✓ Follow the on-screen instructions to simulate the use of Emergency SOS via Satellite.

✓ Upon completing the demo, tap the "End" button in the top right corner.

✓ When prompted, confirm by tapping the "End Demo" button.

Roadside Assistance via Satellite

Let's see another remarkable feature unveiled at the September 2023 Apple Event: Roadside Assistance via Satellite. Initially available in the United States thanks to a partnership between Apple and AAA, this feature is tailored to address issues you might encounter with your vehicle while off-grid, such as a breakdown.

To access this service, you'll need to enroll in a membership with AAA. You can seamlessly utilize this membership in emergencies if you're already a member. Plus, when you purchase an iPhone 15 Pro Max, you'll enjoy complimentary access to these services for two years.

To employ Roadside Assistance via Satellite on your iPhone, follow these straightforward steps:

✓ Send a text message to Roadside Assistance.

✓ A pop-up window will emerge, presenting you with various options to seek help. Choose the option most relevant to your situation, or select "Other Issue" if none of the predefined options fit your needs.

✓ Follow the provided instructions to orient your iPhone towards the nearest satellite.

✓ Ensuring your device has sufficient battery life to use this feature effectively is crucial. Although the iPhone 15 Pro Max boasts significant battery improvements, carrying a charger is always a prudent precaution.

## International Calling and Roaming

International calling and roaming are great when traveling abroad with your iPhone 15 Pro Max.

✓ Making International Calls

Dialing International Numbers: To make international calls, open the Phone app and dial the country code, followed by the local number. For example, dial +33 (country code) and the local number to call a number in France.

International Calling Plan: Check with your mobile carrier to ensure you have an international calling plan or add-on if needed.

✓ Understanding International Roaming

Contact Your Carrier: Contact your mobile carrier to understand international roaming rates and policies before traveling.

Data Roaming: Be aware that data roaming can be costly. Consider turning off data roaming in your settings to avoid unexpected charges.

✓ Managing Data and Call Costs When Traveling

Wi-Fi: Use Wi-Fi networks for data whenever possible to avoid data roaming charges.

Check Data Usage: Monitor your data usage in your iPhone's settings to avoid overages.

Disable Automatic App Updates: Turn off automatic app updates to prevent them from using your data while abroad.

Download Maps Offline: Use apps like Google Maps to download maps for offline use.

Use Messaging Apps: Use messaging apps like WhatsApp, iMessage, or Facebook Messenger for texting and calling over Wi-Fi.

✓ Using Wi-Fi Calling

Enable Wi-Fi Calling: Open the "Settings" app, go to "Phone," and toggle on "Wi-Fi Calling." Follow the on-screen instructions to set it up.

Make Calls Over Wi-Fi: Once Wi-Fi Calling is enabled, your iPhone automatically switches to Wi-Fi for calls when a strong Wi-Fi signal is available.

# CHAPTER THIRTEEN

## Latest Features in iOS 17

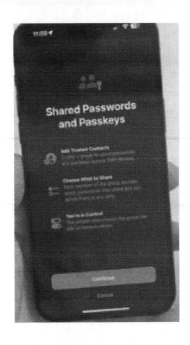

The latest iOS 17 update brings your iPhone many exciting features and enhancements. From a revamped Lock Screen experience to innovative health features, interactive widgets to a more immersive Messages experience, and even offline access to Apple Maps, iOS 17 has something for everyone. Let's look at the top 10 features you should try:

**iPhone StandBy Mode:** Apple has redefined the Lock Screen experience in iOS 17 by introducing the new landscape StandBy mode for iPhones. You now have the flexibility to choose from dual-view options and customize your setup. Additionally, you can select from a range of clock faces that occupy the entire screen, giving your device a fresh and personalized look.

**Messages Stickers and New UI:** Expressing yourself in messages has never been more fun. iOS 17 allows you to respond to text or image messages with emojis or custom stickers, expanding your expressive options beyond the standard tap-back choices. Also, a fresh UI for iMessage apps enhances your messaging experience.

**Screen Distance:** Prioritize your eye health with the new Screen Distance feature. Designed for users of all ages, it helps prevent eye strain and reduces the risk of myopia in children. Setting it up is a breeze, and the results are remarkably effective.

**Offline Apple Maps:** Say goodbye to worries about conserving battery or navigating without a network connection. iOS 17 empowers you to download Apple Maps for offline use, ensuring you never lose your way, even in areas with limited connectivity.

**Shared Passwords:** Sharing passwords with individuals or groups is now effortless. iOS 17 introduces the ability to create shared iCloud Keychain vaults, streamlining password management and enhancing security.

**Automatic 2FA Code Deletion:** Simplify your digital security with iOS 17's automatic deletion of 2FA code texts after they've served their purpose. This feature not only declutters your messages but also enhances your privacy.

**Contact Posters:** iOS 17 takes customization to the next level with Contact Posters. This feature allows you to unleash your creativity by designing unique posters, not only for yourself but also for your contacts. Express your individuality and make your digital interactions more visually appealing.

**Live Voicemail:** Stay in control of your calls with Live Voicemail. Now, you can preview messages left by callers in real-time, enabling you to decide whether to answer without the need to call back. It's a time-saving feature that enhances your communication experience.

**Personal Voice:** Personal Voice is a remarkable capability that ensures your voice is preserved for the future. Whether you're concerned about losing your voice due to a degenerative condition or want to be prepared, Personal Voice lets you create and securely store a backup of your unique voice.

**Interactive Widgets:** Widgets receive a significant upgrade, offering enhanced functionality on your Home or Lock Screen. Access information and perform actions more conveniently with these dynamic widgets.

Go through these exciting features and elevate your iPhone 15 Pro Max experience with iOS 17.

# CONCLUSION

The iPhone 15 Pro Max is Apple's premier smartphone, offering powerful performance, an immersive display, and advanced camera capabilities. With the A17 Pro Bionic processor, 8GB RAM, and up to 1TB storage, it can easily handle demanding apps and multitask. The 6.7-inch OLED Super Retina XDR display provides incredible visuals, made even more immersive by the nearly edge-to-edge screen.

For photography, the 48MP triple camera system takes stunning photos and videos, including portraits, landscapes, and low-light scenes. The LiDAR scanner also enables sophisticated AR experiences.

With 5G connectivity, MagSafe accessories, and iOS 17, the iPhone 15 Pro Max is a top-of-the-line device. While the cost may seem high, Apple has packed this phone with cutting-edge features and longevity, making it a worthwhile investment for those seeking the ultimate iPhone experience.

With care and maintenance, you can enjoy this device for years. For its power, functionality, and innovation combination, the iPhone 15 Pro Max represents the pinnacle of Apple's design.

# ABOUT THE AUTHOR

Curtis Campbell is an intelligent and innovative computer scientist with experience in software engineering. As a renowned technology expert, his passion for capturing still photos and motion pictures has led him into photography and videography, which he is doing with excellence. Curtis has produced several tutorials on different topics. As a researcher and a prolific writer with proficiency in handling tech products, he learned different approaches to managing issues on the internet and other applications.

Made in the USA
Columbia, SC
18 September 2024

859a8fd4-31f5-4ae7-833a-0759f5d9ec50R01